Serious Nonsense

GROUNDHOG LODGES,
VERSAMMLINGE,
AND PENNSYLVANIA
GERMAN HERITAGE

William W. Donner

The Pennsylvania State University Press,
University Park, Pennsylvania

A KEYSTONE BOOK®
Keystone Books are intended to serve the citizens of Pennsylvania. They are accessible, well-researched explorations into the history, culture, society, and environment of the Keystone State as part of the Middle Atlantic region.

Library of Congress Cataloging-in-Publication Data

Names: Donner, William Wilkinson, author.
Title: Serious nonsense : groundhog lodges, Versammlinge, and Pennsylvania German heritage / William W. Donner.
Description: University Park, Pennsylvania : The Pennsylvania State University Press, [2016] | Includes bibliographical references and index.
Summary: "Explores Pennsylvania German versammlinge (meetings), where participants celebrate and preserve their heritage and culture. Argues that these gatherings, conducted in the Pennsylvania German Deitsch language, are rooted in American communicative styles that date back to the late nineteenth and early twentieth centuries, before mass and electronic media"—Provided by publisher.
Identifiers: LCCN 2015038258 | ISBN 9780271071183 (pbk. : alk. paper)
Subjects: LCSH: Pennsylvania Dutch—Social life and customs. | Meetings—Pennsylvania—History.
Classification: LCC F160.G3 D66 2016 | DDC 305.893/10748—dc23
LC record available at http://lccn.loc.gov/2015038258

Copyright © 2016 The Pennsylvania State University
All rights reserved
Printed in the United States of America
Published by The Pennsylvania State University Press,
University Park, PA 16802-1003

The Pennsylvania State University Press is a member of the Association of American University Presses.

It is the policy of The Pennsylvania State University Press to use acid-free paper. Publications on uncoated stock satisfy the minimum requirements of American National Standard for Information Sciences—Permanence of Paper for Printed Library Material, ANSI Z39.48–1992.

Frontispiece: A large groundhog is brought into Groundhog Lodge #1, 1971. A man inside stops and chats with different people in the audience. Photo: *Allentown Morning Call*. All rights reserved.

Additional credits: Pages xvi, 8, 24, 46, 62, 78, 98, and 124 show various years of program covers for Groundhog Lodge #1. Courtesy of author.

Contents

List of Illustrations........................ vii

Preface ix

Introduction 1

1. The People and Language That the Versammlinge Celebrate 9

2. Making Tradition: The Origins and Development of the Versammlinge 25

3. "Let Us *Deitsche* Be What We Are": The Structure of Versammling Events 47

4. Theatricality: Performing Tradition..... 63

5. The Message of the Versammlinge: The Reverend Clarence Rahn and the Main Speech................................ 79

6. Region and Nation: Contexts for the Versammling Movement 99

7. The Future of Pennsylvania Germans and Their Versammlinge 125

Notes..................................... 133

Glossary 145

Bibliography.............................. 147

Index..................................... 159

Illustrations

Illustrations follow p. 96

1. First meeting of Groundhog Lodge #1 in Allentown, February 2, 1934
2. *Raad* (board) of Groundhog Lodge #2 watching groundhog, ca. 1950
3. *Ferbinnerei* (*Verbinnerei*), oath of membership, Groundhog Lodge #1, 1972
4. *Ferbinnerei* (*Verbinnerei*), oath of membership, Groundhog Lodge #2, ca. 1955
5. Crowning the groundhog, 1968
6. Back cover of program for Groundhog Lodge #1, 1939
7. Rev. Rahn speaking at Groundhog Lodge #2, ca. 1944
8. Illustration from program for Groundhog Lodge #1, 1942
9. New Year's Wish, Groundhog Lodge #1, 1943
10. Meeting announcement and invitation for Groundhog Lodge #1, 2011
11. Admission ticket for Groundhog Lodge #1 meeting, 2011
12. *Taufschein* (*Daafschein*), or baptism certificate, commemorating the first organizational meeting of Groundhog Lodge #1 in 1933
13. Pennsylvania German flag
14. Sign hanging at front of meetings of Groundhog Lodge #1: "English Shwetza Is Ferbotta" (Speaking English is forbidden)
15. Mounted animal scene from the front of speaker's stand, Groundhog Lodge #1
16. Eight-foot-tall groundhog statue at the front of every meeting of Groundhog Lodge #1

17 *Raad* (wheel) listing the members of the board of Groundhog Lodge #1 in 2015

18 View of meeting of Groundhog Lodge #1 at Germansville Fire Company, 2013

19 "Schnitzelbank" song from the back covers of Lodge #1 programs

20 Band at Groundhog Lodge #1, 2015

21 Procession bringing in a stuffed groundhog to be placed at the podium, Groundhog Lodge #1, 2013

22 The thirteen members of the *Raad* (board) of Groundhog Lodge #1, standing in front of the large groundhog, 2005

23 *Ferbinnerei (Verbinnerei)*, oath of membership, Lodge #1, 2015

24 Program cover for Groundhog Lodge #1, 1958

25 Program cover for Groundhog Lodge #1, 1962

26 Program cover for Groundhog Lodge #1, 1965

27 Program cover for Groundhog Lodge #1, 1970

28 Program cover for Groundhog Lodge #1, 1979

29 Program cover for Groundhog Lodge #1, 1999

30 Rev. Rahn gives the main speech in front of a coffin for the goose, a weather-predicting rival of the groundhog, Groundhog Lodge #1, 1970

31 Women protest that they cannot attend meetings, Groundhog Lodge #1, 1973

32 Performers at Groundhog Lodge #2, ca. 1965

33 Local television crew interviewing Bill Meck, dressed as a groundhog, and Groundhog Lodge #1 leader (*Haaptmann*) Bill Williams, 2013

34 Doctor giving an injection during a skit, Groundhog Lodge #1, 2013

35 Groundhog being brought across the Jordan Creek, Lehigh County, 2013

Preface

I had a circuitous route to this project. Many of my ancestors were Pennsylvania Germans of one form or another. But I was raised in the suburbs of Philadelphia after World War II, and my relationship with Pennsylvania German culture was remote. Whenever I asked about my ancestry, my parents said that it was mostly "German," "Pennsylvania Dutch," or "Pennsylvania German." My parents themselves were quite removed from the culture and people. Certainly none of us had ever heard of the versammlinge, the ceremonial Pennsylvania German "meetings" where only the Pennsylvania German Deitsch language can be spoken, or their most theatrical expression in the groundhog lodge meetings. As an adult, I listened for the first time to my mother's stories about her grandfather, who had been born in Womelsdorf, Berks County, shortly after the Civil War and migrated to Philadelphia as a young man to work on the railroad. She was raised in his house in Elkins Park outside of Philadelphia, and in her childhood she accompanied him on trips to Womelsdorf, in the heart of Pennsylvania German country. My mother probably told me about this throughout my childhood, but I never paid attention to any of it until I was in my late thirties and living in the Pennsylvania German region. When I was in my forties and well into learning about the Pennsylvania Germans, my parents also told me that when I was young we made some family trips to Pennsylvania German sites, including museums and folk festivals. I have absolutely no recollection of these trips. I assume that I must have been completely bored by the museums and events that I was seeing, as I was on other "educational" family trips.

There were a few mementos of Pennsylvania German heritage in my parents' house. There was an old blanket chest, inherited from my great-great grandmother from Lebanon County on which my mother had painted some Pennsylvania German designs in the late 1940s, before I was born.

There were passing references to Pennsylvania Germans in my schooldays, and a second grade Mother's Day class project, probably in 1958, when we painted a picture of a distelfink on bed trays for our mothers. I have a vague memory of hearing a family story about some ancestor who came to hate apple butter for her entire life because that was all there was to eat at some point in her youth. In my mother's kitchen there was a Scotch tape dispenser with a popular Pennsylvania German proverb on the side: "We grow old too soon and smart too late." I also remember taking a group of friends on a trip through Pennsylvania German country during my college years; when we stopped by my parents' house, my mother gave me a high school term paper that she had written in the late 1930s about the Pennsylvania Germans for us to read on our trip.

But beyond a few pieces of furniture, some distinctive food, and some very general references to ancestry and the people, I was not brought up in Pennsylvania German culture. Perhaps worse for my attachment to my ancestry, I grew up in the 1950s after a major war with Germany, and I felt no pride in having anything to do with something that had the word "German" in it. One of my lasting childhood memories is playing "guns and ammo" with neighborhood boys and the bigger kids making us smaller kids take the roles of "Germans," knowing we had to lose. I also vividly remember a neighborhood kid with a German-sounding name, whom I did not know well but who seemed just like the rest of us, being called a "fat Kraut" by the older boys, and hoping no one found anything "German" in my ancestry.

My understanding of Pennsylvania Germans was further confused by the large tourist industry in Lancaster County and popular media. I was left with the completely misinformed image of Pennsylvania Germans as a convoluted caricature of the Old Order Amish: a people who were overweight, were farmers, liked to eat apple butter, spoke fractured English, resisted modern technology, and had strong religious convictions. They were people I had absolutely no interest in. In college I fell in love with my anthropology courses and eventually studied anthropology as a graduate student at the University of Pennsylvania. Although I knew that there were experts on Pennsylvania German culture in the neighboring Department of Folklore and Folklife at Penn—including Don Yoder, in my

Preface

opinion the preeminent scholar—I had no interest in taking any of those courses. I was interested in Oceania and eventually did over three years of ethnographic research between 1980 and 1987 on Sikaiana, a small, isolated island in the Solomon Islands.[1]

In 1988, I had a Ph.D. and, like many other anthropologists, no job. Having lived on a small island in the Pacific with 250 people for several years, I had become interested in how people develop and maintain a sense of community in a small society where everyone knows one another. I decided to see how small communities are organized in the United States and if they have some of the intensity of interactions that I found in my research on Sikaiana. I did not know where to start, although I had always been curious about the social life of the little towns in Pennsylvania that I drove through to various destinations. My mother, who had been doing research on her genealogy, was talking a lot about Womelsdorf, where her grandfather had been raised. Finally a bell went off and I paid attention to what she was saying.

With no other idea of where to learn about small American communities, I moved to a location close to Womelsdorf. I knew I was moving into Pennsylvania German country, but I was not going to study Pennsylvania Germans, mostly because I felt overwhelmed by the size of the literature about them. I was going to study small-town life, which just happened to be in a Pennsylvania German region. I took a job as a waiter in a banquet hall to pay the bills and signed on as a part-time correspondent with a regional newspaper to learn more about the area.[2]

I eventually found a part-time job teaching at a neighboring university, Kutztown University, then another part-time job at Millersville University, outside of Lancaster, and eventually the Kutztown job became full-time. At some point, I decided I should learn more about the Pennsylvania Germans themselves. Teachers know that the best way to learn about a topic is to teach a course about it, so I planned to offer a course about Pennsylvania Germans. In my research I found out that Kutztown University was established in 1866 by Pennsylvania German educators to train Pennsylvania German teachers, although this had little effect on the regional university when I arrived in 1988. My research initially looked at Pennsylvania Germans in the nineteenth century, including the educational policies

of the people who taught at Kutztown University (then Keystone State Normal School). I began to understand more about the people and also to see that their educators changed over the course of the nineteenth century, initially resisting and then later supporting educational policies that emphasized the use of English and assimilation at the same time that they developed new ways to express their distinctive ethnic identity.[3]

I also listened for the first time to my mother recounting her stories of visits to Womelsdorf. I paid attention when she talked about her grandfather's stories of visits from Belsnickle, an old Pennsylvania German tradition in which a disguised Christmas visitor dressed in furs and rags frightens and then rewards Pennsylvania German children (her grandfather suspected it might be his mother in disguise). I also listened to her for the first time when she speculated that her grandfather's trips to Womelsdorf might have been motivated by the desire to see a powwow doctor, a practitioner of a form of alternative healing that was still widely practiced in the 1920s and 1930s when my mother visited. I noticed that my mother liked to make annual trips to the Kutztown Folk Festival.[4] As I learned more, I came to see that her high school term paper about Pennsylvania Germans and the painting of Pennsylvania German designs on her great-grandmother's chest were not only about her ancestry; these activities were also part of a regional and nationwide interest in Pennsylvania German culture that had developed in the 1930s and 1940s.

Once I felt that I actually had some expertise about a few areas of Pennsylvania German life, I began to work with Dr. David Valuska, who at the time was director of the new Pennsylvania German Cultural Heritage Center at Kutztown University. The Center had been recently established to build ties with the local community and exhibit Pennsylvania German materials that the university acquired. Valuska was also an outsider to the culture, but he was brilliant in building the Center by developing ties with a range of community groups. He sent me to my first versammling meeting in the late 1990s. It was a meeting of a groundhog lodge, which has a special emphasis on the groundhog's legendary ability to predict the coming of spring. I was enthralled. There was an eight-foot statue of a groundhog at the front of the room, and men were singing songs, performing humorous skits, laughing, and giving reverence to the groundhog. All this

Preface

was done in the Pennsylvania German Deitsch language. I was surprised and intrigued that culture and heritage were being displayed with such theatricality in modern, industrialized America. Thus began my fascination with the origins and development of these versammlinge.

I was intrigued with the versammlinge as performative events. I also had another academic interest based on my research in the Solomon Islands. Many ethnic groups and regional populations celebrate, if not preserve, their heritage in a rapidly changing and modernizing world. The Sikaiana people, like many Pacific Islanders, had experienced enormous cultural change in the twentieth century and had developed a variety of events and institutions to celebrate their cultural traditions. They danced them, sang them, recorded them, and at special events presented them to outsiders. Like many other indigenous peoples and regional cultures, the Pennsylvania Germans are doing things to celebrate their cultural identity in the midst of rapid change. For a variety of personal and academic reasons, I wanted to learn more about the versammlinge.

There were seventeen active groundhog lodges that had banded together to form a "Grossdaadi Lodge" (Grandfather Lodge) and were interested in recording the history of the groundhog lodges and their annual versammlinge. I began to work with them, and they were an immense help in this project. They keep extensive records of their activities and made them available to me. I read regional newspapers that reported about the activities of the versammlinge. I learned that there were several variations of versammlinge, some centered on the groundhog, others including many similar elements but without the ceremony of the groundhog, and although I kept a primary focus on the groundhog lodges, I expanded my research to include other kinds of versammlinge. Many Pennsylvania Germans gave freely of their time to talk with me. Those involved in the versammlinge and their close family members are interested in recording an important expression of their culture that they fear will be lost in another generation. After learning more about the versammlinge, my research went in unexpected directions as I found that I needed to contextualize these events in broader trends in American theater, humor, and regional literature. This book is the culmination of an academic journey to learn about the expression of ethnic identity in American society and a personal journey to learn

more about my heritage as someone with Pennsylvania German ancestors. In learning about my Pennsylvania German heritage, I also learned a lot about my heritage as an American.

I could not have written this book without the help and encouragement of many people and organizations. For a number of years I have been a Commonwealth Speaker for the Pennsylvania Humanities Council. In this capacity, I have gone to many different towns and communities in southeastern Pennsylvania and given talks about the versammlinge. I am grateful for the feedback people have given me on these talks. I also have been involved with a variety of heritage organizations, including the Kutztown Folk Festival, the Pennsylvania German Society, and the Pennsylvania German Cultural Heritage Center at Kutztown University, all of which have important relationships with participants in the versammlinge who helped me understand the events. I was appointed as an honorary member of the board of directors (*Raad*) of Groundhog Lodge #1, and more recently a board member, and I have become involved in their preparations for their annual meetings. I have also benefitted from the resources of many different institutions, including the special collections and libraries at Millersville University, Franklin and Marshall College, Muhlenberg College, Ursinus College, the Lehigh County Historical Society, the Allentown Public Library, the Snyder County Historical Society, Historic Schaefferstown Inc., the Lancaster Theological Seminary, the Pennsylvania German Society, and the Pennsylvania German Cultural Heritage Center at Kutztown University. Many people helped by providing me with materials about the history of the versammlinge; I am especially indebted to Carl Snyder, Clarence Heffendrager, Ruth and Richard Schaefer, Ron Treichler, Richard Savidge, Leonard Shupp, and the board of Groundhog Lodge #1.

I have been blessed with some very patient Pennsylvania Germans who have taken their time to explain to me their culture and activities. Some people claim that Pennsylvania Germans can be stubborn and somewhat wary of outsiders. But I have found them to be kind and helpful beyond anything I deserve. They have been very reliable in replying to my inquiries, far more than I have in responding to theirs. Again, if this book has any merit, the many people who shared some moments of their lives with me should receive the credit.

I am very grateful to a number of people who read various versions of the book and provided very helpful advice, including Ruth Schaefer, Paul Kunkel, Donald Breininger, Carl Snyder, Ron Treichler, Richard Miller, Patrick Donmoyer, Richard Wolf, Robert Kline, Jennifer Schlegel, Russell Heintzelman, and my two sons, Bill and Phillip Donner. Ed Quinter and Patrick Donmoyer provided help with details about the Pennsylvania German Deitsch language; Mark Louden also gave me helpful comments about Deitsch and shared some chapters of a book that he is writing about the language. At Penn State, two anonymous reviewers provided useful suggestions. Kathryn Yahner, the series editor, was a source of support and encouragement throughout the publication process, and I am very grateful for her guidance and her staff for their help. I am also very grateful to John Morris, manuscript editor at Penn State Press, for making very helpful editorial comments and corrections. If this book has any merit, the people mentioned above should be given much of the credit; any failings are solely my responsibility.

Introduction

I attended my first Pennsylvania German *Versammling* (meeting) sometime in the late 1990s in Northampton, a small town about ten miles north of Allentown, Pennsylvania. Men gathered together to celebrate their Pennsylvania German life and heritage and to praise the legendary ability of the groundhog to predict the arrival of spring. The event was highly theatrical and ceremonial. There were three or four hundred men in the hall. At the front were a decorated stage and an eight-foot statue of a groundhog wearing a crown. At the beginning of the meeting, everyone stood reverently as men in top hats carried in a stuffed groundhog and placed it in front of the speaker's podium. They pledged allegiance to the American flag, sang "America," and then listened to a prayer, all in the Pennsylvania German Deitsch language. They raised both hands as paws and took an oath of allegiance to the lodge and groundhog; they listened to a weather report, piped into the speaker system, about whether or not the groundhog saw his shadow; they ate a hearty meal; they sang songs; they watched a humorous skit about a lecherous doctor who cured people by transferring their ailments to his assistant; and they listened to an inspirational

talk, sprinkled with humor, about the values of Pennsylvania German life. Anyone who spoke English, especially from the podium, was charged a fine for each word (see figures 18, 21).

Thousands of meetings like this one have been held in the Pennsylvania German region since the early 1930s, when the automobile made movement both into and within the area much easier, electronic mass media began replacing the regional and local interpersonal performances that the meetings preserve, outsiders began to admire Pennsylvania Germans, and Pennsylvania Germans themselves wanted to revive pride in their heritage after the anti-German sentiment of World War I. There are several variations of versammlinge (-e ending for the plural form). Some, like the one described above, are restricted to males and center on legends about the groundhog's weather-predicting abilities. I will refer to these as "groundhog lodges." Others are generally open to both men and women and do not feature a groundhog ceremony. I will refer to these as "general versammlinge."[1] All the meetings celebrate Pennsylvania German language and heritage in an evening of entertainment and fellowship. Unfortunately, while everyone has heard of Punxsutawney Phil, whose weather prognostications are followed by news media throughout the country and have even provided the inspiration for a Hollywood movie, the versammlinge are little known to people outside the Pennsylvania German regions and even to many within it. Most Americans know something about the horses and buggies of the Old Order Amish, but few know about the "fancy" or "Church" Pennsylvania Germans, who are mostly Lutheran and German Reformed and who preserve their cultural traditions in events like the versammlinge at the same time that they use modern technology and participate in the broader American society. This is a shame because the versammlinge represent one of the most interesting expressions of ethnic identity and language preservation in America.

This book is about the origins, development, and activities of these meetings. It is also an examination of the development and expression of Pennsylvania German ethnic identity in the twentieth and twenty-first centuries. The versammlinge are part of a broader movement in which Pennsylvania Germans have combined elements of their own heritage with elements of American experience to express an ethnic identity within

the context of a larger social system in which technology, media, and social life are constantly changing. I hope that this book will introduce readers to Pennsylvania German practices that tourists rarely see, and that outsiders, including academics, rarely learn about.

The title of this book is derived from a statement by Clarence Rahn, a German Reformed pastor who was the most popular speaker at versammlinge until his death in 1977. Responding to criticisms of the apparent nonsense of the groundhog lodge meetings, Rahn described them in the Pennsylvania German Deitsch language as *verschtennich dummheeda*, which he translated as "sensible nonsense" and defined, in a 1975 talk, as the many things that people do, like meetings in hunting lodges, sports events, and other social gatherings, that seem foolish, with little practical value, but that are important in creating a sense of "fellowship." Fellowship is very important for the participants in all versammlinge. I also think the versammlinge are an important expression of Pennsylvania German heritage and identity, an occasion to maintain both a language and style of expression, and an opportunity to examine both the past and present. There is serious content in a lot that seems to be nonsense.[2]

I first set out to write this book for Pennsylvania Germans themselves, but in the process of writing it, I found that the origins of the lodges were a regional expression of more general themes in American life, especially literary, humorous, and theatrical traditions in the nineteenth century. I decided to write this book for a broader audience. This book is still for those familiar with these events, and perhaps more importantly, it is for their children and grandchildren so they can understand what was accomplished and expressed at the gatherings. It is also for scholars in many fields who study ethnicity, language and cultural history, preservation and change. Finally, I hope to reach a general audience of people outside of academia who are interested in Pennsylvania Germans and in an American ethnic group that has preserved and developed distinctive cultural practices in a rapidly changing society.

Most Americans have distorted and misleading images of Pennsylvania Germans that are derived from a conflation of a highly commercialized tourist industry centered on the Old Order Amish, an eighteenth-century craft tradition that has become collectible, and superficial images in

American media and culture. For the first forty years of my life I was one of those people, even though I have Pennsylvania German ancestors and grew up within an hour's drive of Pennsylvania German regions. I was never sure whether the people were "Pennsylvania German," "Pennsylvania Dutch," or "German American," nor did I understand how the Amish and Plain People fit into those people. I assumed my ancestors were Old Order Amish (they were not), although it all seemed very remote from my middle-class life and mostly secular parents. Popular culture, tourism literature, mass media, and even members of my family presented the Pennsylvania German language as something mongrel, either an inferior "lower" form of "High" German or some ridiculous combination of English and German.[3] Worse, I was a baby boomer who grew up under the shadow of a major war with Germany and was not proud of having ancestry with the word "German" in it.

It was not until I was an adult with a Ph.D. in anthropology, had a teaching job in the region, and decided to do research about the people in the region where I lived that I began to understand more about the Pennsylvania Germans and about the sources for my many misunderstandings. I learned that there are some significant differences between Pennsylvania Germans and other German Americans. I learned that the Old Order groups are a small minority of the people who are labeled as Pennsylvania German and that, contrary to popular understandings, these groups have changed over time. I came to understand that the great majority of Pennsylvania Germans, the "Church" or "fancy" people, have largely participated in American life, interacting with others, contributing to American culture and drawing from it. And as the world around them has changed, they have constantly redefined themselves and their relations with others, while continuing to maintain and develop expressions of their culture and heritage throughout the nineteenth and into the twentieth and twenty-first centuries.

In describing the versammlinge, I focus on the activities of Groundhog Lodge #1, the oldest groundhog lodge, which was formed in 1933 and held its first meeting in 1934. It became the model and inspiration for most of the other versammlinge, both the groundhog lodges and the general versammlinge. I interviewed many of the people involved in all kinds of versammlinge, including leaders, active participants, popular speakers,

and skit writers. I attended meetings and other public events. Beginning with the versammlinge's first formation in the 1930s, regional newspapers often described the events at these gatherings, and I read microfilms of these newspapers. Participants in the gatherings often kept programs and records of these meetings, and this was another important source of information. Early in my research, I was told that the main speaker or banquet speech (*Fescht Rade*, *Feschtred*) was a very important event at the meetings and that Clarence Rahn (1898–1977) was the preeminent speaker, combining both humor and a message in his speeches. Rahn influenced a generation of speakers, and I was able to interview many of them. I also interviewed Rahn's daughter and son-in-law, Richard and Ruth Schaefer. In the regional press, Rahn was often compared to Mark Twain and Will Rogers. This led me to take a harder look at American humor traditions and popular culture in the nineteenth and early twentieth centuries. I began to recognize some of the humor in the lodges as reflecting themes in nineteenth-century Pennsylvania German humorous writing, which itself, I learned, was influenced by broader trends in American literature and popular culture.

In writing this book, I have tried to show the excitement and drama of the meetings. Many of my interviews were tape-recorded, and I have liberally quoted from my interviews, letting the versammling participants speak for themselves, which I found they did passionately and eloquently. In some cases, quotes come from the past, from people I could not talk with directly but whose statements are recorded in regional newspapers and documents. To give readers a more intimate and visual sense of what happens at meetings, I have also included examples of the events that take place, excerpts from skits and speeches, and pictures.

I am not fluent in the Pennsylvania German Deitsch language, although I can read and understand some, and for much of this book I rely upon the statements and translations of people who are fluent and who were raised in a more visible and immediate Pennsylvania German culture. My own translations have been checked with people who are knowledgeable. These consultants and informants, like all participants in versammlinge, are fluent English speakers themselves and live in a largely English-speaking world.[4]

This book emphasizes several major themes. First, I want to show how a tradition was created. The versammlinge were not a cultural practice of the eighteenth-century German settlers who became the ancestors of the versammling participants. The meetings were created in the 1930s as a new way to celebrate tradition, and, over the course of several decades, they became traditional themselves. Second, in a related vein, I want to describe how Pennsylvania German ethnicity developed in the twentieth century and continues to develop into the present. Although many people think of ethnic identity as primordial, static, and about the past, it changes over time and is continually redefined as the larger societal and cultural contexts change. Third, I want to show how the meetings are related to broader themes in American culture. Much of their content is derived from American late nineteenth- and early twentieth-century oral and theatrical traditions, and often expresses American cultural traditions that emphasize the humor and wisdom of the common person. The versammlinge illustrate that Pennsylvania Germans have constantly defined their ethnicity and heritage in ways that are both distinctive and also part of general currents in American culture.

In this book, the terms "heritage," "ethnicity," and "ethnic identity" will have loose and overlapping meanings. "Heritage" refers to an attachment and celebration of practices associated with ancestry or cultural traditions. "Ethnicity" refers generally to practices that are shared among a group of people, often based on shared ancestry or cultural traditions. Heritage is more about the past, while ethnicity is more about the present, although heritage is defined in the present as people assess and reassess their past. "Ethnic identity" is a sense of self derived from belonging to a particular ethnicity. The meanings and implications of the processes associated with these terms are constantly changing and being redefined through experience and interactions with others, although the members of an ethnic group often assume a more static and stable meaning for these terms. To be sure, these terms themselves were developed by social scientists in the twentieth century, and their meanings are still changing for the social scientists who use them. I use these terms far more frequently in this book than I ever heard Pennsylvania Germans do when talking among themselves. Nevertheless, I think they correspond with important

processes and understandings that Pennsylvania Germans share, especially in terms of their involvement with the versammlinge.

Chapter 1 discusses the background to the study by clarifying misunderstandings and dispelling false stereotypes about Pennsylvania Germans and their language and culture. Usually, this kind of discussion is placed in an introduction. But since many readers, including some with advanced academic backgrounds, may have images of Pennsylvania Germans similar to the distorted ones I once had, I believe these issues must be part of the main discussion. Chapter 2 describes the origin and spread of the versammlinge, which started in the 1930s and over the next fifty years became widely popular through the Pennsylvania German regions. At present, however, the movement is in decline because of the loss of people who can speak the Pennsylvania German Deitsch language. Chapter 3 examines the activities that take place during the versammlinge, which have remained remarkably constant across the many different gatherings for over eighty years. Chapter 4 describes the theatricality and drama that are an essential part of the versammlinge, and how that theatricality reflects nineteenth-century American dramatic conventions while also incorporating contemporary concerns. Chapter 5 examines the speeches that are given at the versammlinge, which, both through style and content, deliver meaningful messages. This chapter focuses on the Reverend Clarence Rahn, who is considered the exemplary speaker and in many respects represents the quintessential Pennsylvania German of the twentieth century. Chapter 6 looks at the broader trends in American culture and in Pennsylvania German life that provided the historical and social context for the development of the versammlinge. The versammlinge originated at a time when Pennsylvania Germans were expressing their heritage in many different events, which should be understood in the broader context of a national interest in regional cultures. Chapter 7 concludes by discussing the accomplishments of the versammlinge and some of their possible futures.

One of my most important goals in writing this book is to help others understand more about Pennsylvania Germans and what they have accomplished. In this respect, I am writing this book for someone like myself about twenty-five years ago, with a totally confused and inaccurate conception of Pennsylvania Germans.

1.

The People and Language That the Versammlinge Celebrate

⟶

Versammling, often written *fersommling*, is the Pennsylvania German word for "gathering" or "meeting" or religious "congregation," and is commonly used to refer to special occasions when several hundred Pennsylvania Germans come together to celebrate their heritage and language. Since the first meeting in 1933, there have been thousands of these gatherings in southeastern Pennsylvania, and about forty are still held every year now, in the second decade of the twenty-first century. The prayers, pledges, songs, skits, speeches, and humor are presented in a highly ceremonial and dramatic format, all in the Pennsylvania German Deitsch language. Nineteenth-century American dramatic and humorous traditions are used to comment on current events. A common theme is the contrast between a simpler but naïve past and a complex and perplexing present. Combining important themes of both American and Pennsylvania German culture, these gatherings represent an expression of an ethnic tradition with origins in the eighteenth century that has been maintained and developed over the past three hundred years. Although largely unknown to academics, they are an example of how an ethnic group has participated in the

larger American society, both contributing and assimilating to it while still preserving its cultural traditions. More than many other immigrant groups, including other German Americans, Pennsylvania Germans have not only maintained but also developed traditions that preserved and celebrated their distinctive ethnicity. The versammlinge are foremost among these traditions.

To understand the significance of these versammlinge for Pennsylvania Germans and for American ethnic life more generally, it is necessary to first understand the background of the people at these events, the heritage that they are celebrating, and the language that they insist on using.

Who Are the Pennsylvania Germans?

Some of the confusion about Pennsylvania Germans includes the various terms that are used to refer to them: the "Pennsylvania Germans" and "Pennsylvania Dutch" are the same group of people. Most are the descendants of immigrants from a region called the Palatinate, in and around the southwestern part of what is now Germany along the Rhine River (Germany was not a nation when these immigrants left their homeland). The immigration started in the late 1600s and continued through the eighteenth century. Pennsylvania German/Dutch culture and language were formed in the United States during the eighteenth century, and they continued to evolve and change during the nineteenth and twentieth centuries.

As with many ethnic terms, there is a sometimes nasty debate about whether Pennsylvania "German" or "Dutch" is the best term for this group of people. "Pennsylvania German" is used by those who do not want to be confused with the Holland Dutch and want to emphasize the Germanic origins of the Pennsylvania Germans. "Pennsylvania Dutch" is preferred by those who emphasize that the people refer to themselves in their everyday vernacular as *Pennsilfaanisch Deitsch*, and do not want to be identified with a German nationality that formed after their ancestors migrated (some Pennsylvania Germans have Swiss, Alsatian, and French ancestry). Generally, wealthier people and professionals who know "High" (Standard) German will prefer "Pennsylvania German," while farmers and working-class people, as well as some academics, will prefer "Pennsylvania Dutch."[1]

In the colloquial usage of people in the region, those residents who are imbued with Pennsylvania German/Dutch qualities in manner and accent are usually referred to as "Dutchy," not "Pennsylvania German." Sometimes I have heard people who consider themselves to be "Pennsylvania Dutch" use "Pennsylvania German" to refer to a group that might be called "Germans in Pennsylvania," that is, the descendants of Germans who migrated into the region in the 1800s and 1900s, after the Pennsylvania German/Dutch settlements were well established. This more recent group was often quite different from the existing population and sometimes had prickly relations with them. Many of my students from the region tell me that they never heard "Pennsylvania German" before taking my class in "Pennsylvania German Studies"; they only heard "Dutch." On the other hand, the oldest and most important society for studying the Pennsylvania Germans/Dutch is the Pennsylvania German Society, founded in 1891. At the society's first meeting there was a debate about whether it should be the "Pennsylvania German" or the "Pennsylvania Dutch" Society. The majority of the society's founders were from wealthy and professional backgrounds, and "Pennsylvania German" prevailed. When I was on the board of that society in the early twenty-first century, the members of the board still strongly preferred "Pennsylvania German." I once heard a respected board member, fluent in the language and active in versammlinge, complain that everything bad about Pennsylvania German activities came from the people who use the term "Pennsylvania Dutch." As an editor of several regional journals, I have received letters that adamantly argued for the exclusive use of each term. For many years, I have been involved with the Pennsylvania German Cultural Heritage Center, which absorbed most of its collections from the Pennsylvania Dutch Folk Culture Society. The participants in the versammlinge are split in their preference, although at this point I suspect that a majority use "Dutch" to refer to themselves. My mother, with ancestral roots in the area, seems to have been confused on this issue as well. Her high school term paper about the Pennsylvania Germans, briefly mentioned in this book's preface, was entitled "The Pennsylvania Germans," but she used both "Pennsylvania Dutch" and "Pennsylvania German" in the paper without any consistent pattern of usage.

For the title of this book, I decided on "Pennsylvania German." I fear that for most of my audience outside of the region, "Pennsylvania Dutch" will be misleading, calling forth images of Holland, and if I used the preferable term "Deitsch," no one would know what the book is about. Nonetheless, I have considerable sympathy for the use of "Pennsylvania Dutch," since I think it reflects the value this culture places on the people most likely to use this term, the common people—whose importance is a major theme in the versammlinge.

Although Germans who migrated to Pennsylvania and the rest of the states in the nineteenth and twentieth centuries did have some interactions with the Pennsylvania Germans, most scholars and most Pennsylvania Germans themselves, whether they prefer "Pennsylvania German" or "Pennsylvania Dutch," think of these more recent immigrants as different. Indeed, many of them were. The latter group often spoke Standard or "High" German as opposed to the Pennsylvania German Deitsch language, they were more involved in an industrial as opposed to an agricultural economy, they usually immigrated to urban as opposed to rural areas, and they often had a much stronger connection to the developing German nation. When the Pennsylvania German Society was founded in 1891, it limited full membership to descendants of the people who arrived in Pennsylvania in the late 1600s and 1700s from Germanic regions, especially the southwestern part of what is now the modern German nation and neighboring regions. Like many ancestral organizations in the late nineteenth century, when there was heavy immigration from many different parts of Europe into the United States, the Pennsylvania Germans, whose ancestors had fought in the French and Indian War and the War of Independence, wanted to assert their roots in early colonial American experience.[2]

There is more than simple ancestral chauvinism, however, to the assertion that Pennsylvania Germans were and remain different from later-arriving German Americans. Most scholars agree that between 1700 and 1800, Pennsylvania Germans developed a language and culture that had German roots, especially in the regions around Pfalz or the Palatinate along the Upper Rhine, and was also shaped by life in both Europe and America through interactions with other Americans. Thus,

their language and culture were derived from a variety of different sources in both Germany and America and then constructed here in America. Although they considered themselves more American than the later-arriving Germans, the Pennsylvania Germans would develop and maintain their subculture far longer. The versammlinge themselves are examples of this American cultural development. Most of the activities and ceremonies in the versammlinge—indeed, the idea for the versammlinge themselves—developed from Pennsylvania German experience here in the United States.

Pennsylvania Germans are commonly seen as falling into two rough categories: the "Sect" people, including Anabaptists or "Plain" people, and the "Church," or "fancy" or "gay," people. The Church people, who make up over 90 percent of all Pennsylvania Germans, are predominantly Lutherans and German Reformed (now United Church of Christ), although a number of them (including some of my ancestors) converted to a form of Methodism in the late eighteenth and early nineteenth centuries. While maintaining many Pennsylvania German cultural practices, the Church people constantly adopted new technology and participated in many ways in the contemporaneous, and also continually changing, American culture. These Church people are the great majority of people who participate in versammlinge.[3]

The Anabaptist groups include Amish, Mennonites, and Brethren, and these denominations in turn include many different groups with varying beliefs and practices. The most well known are probably the Old Order Amish, with their horses-and-buggies and distinctive dress and practices; indeed, many people from outside the region probably associate Pennsylvania Germans in general with the Old Order Amish. But in fact they (along with the Old Order Mennonites and a few other technologically conservative Anabaptists) are a minority among the Anabaptists, and a very small minority among all Pennsylvania Germans, and are not involved in the versammlinge. The distinctiveness of the Old Order Anabaptists became emphasized in the late nineteenth century as Amish and Mennonite groups splintered over how to preserve religious values in an industrializing society (the Amish were originally a seventeenth-century splinter group from the Mennonites). Today Old Order

and other conservative Anabaptists come in many varieties and gradations, but they generally maintain a distinctive lifestyle that filters, if not rejects, many modern practices and large segments of modern technology. They make up the great majority of the people who actively maintain the Pennsylvania German Deitsch language as the primary language at home. Most Anabaptists, however, including most Mennonites and Brethren and some groups of Amish, are not members of Old Order groups and are hard to distinguish from the general American population. They dress in modern styles, drive cars, and use modern technology, although they remain committed to Anabaptist principles, including pacifism, adult baptism, and a modest lifestyle.[4]

The first immigrants who came to be thought of as Pennsylvania Germans arrived in 1683 and formed a settlement near Philadelphia which to this day is called Germantown.[5] Later migrants settled in a semi-arc in the areas around Philadelphia, including what are now Montgomery, Chester, Bucks, Berks, Northampton, Lehigh, Schuylkill, Lebanon, and Lancaster Counties. Subsequently, there was movement to adjacent counties and states: there are significant Pennsylvania German settlements in Dauphin, York, Northumberland, Union, and Snyder Counties, on both sides of the Susquehanna River about a hundred miles west of Philadelphia, and in the Shenandoah Valley deep into Virginia. Pennsylvania Germans migrated to Canada in 1786 and still celebrate their Pennsylvania German heritage. Census materials and records of language use in schools indicate that in the middle of the nineteenth century by far the highest concentrations of Church Pennsylvania Germans were in Lehigh and Berks Counties, with high concentrations of Mennonites in Lancaster County.

The first recorded versammling took place in 1933, in Selinsgrove, Snyder County, on the west bank of the Susquehanna River, and today there is still a very active versammling on the other side of the Susquehanna River in Lykens, Dauphin County. The strongest area for the versammlinge, however, is centered about seventy miles east, in and around Lehigh and Berks Counties.

The people who participate in versammlinge and are described in this book have retained the language and usually have roots in rural or small-town life. Most are Church Pennsylvania Germans. Old Order and

culturally "conservative" Anabaptists rarely, if ever, participate in these events. My view is that Old Order people, and Anabaptists more generally, have a strong allegiance to a religious set of values and a weak, if any, allegiance to a secular Pennsylvania German identity. The people who attend versammlinge are usually committed Christians, but they also have a strong allegiance to a secular identity as Pennsylvania Germans.[6]

The Language: Deitsch

Versammlinge are structured around the use of the Pennsylvania German language. Like so much else about Pennsylvania Germans, their language was derived from Europe and shaped in America. Their ancestors arrived in Pennsylvania speaking related dialects of German, specifically the regional dialects spoken in the regions in and around southwest Germany in the late seventeenth and eighteenth centuries. These dialects merged in America to create Deitsch, the term that Pennsylvania Germans use for their language and that I will use in this book.[7] Deitsch is a dialect or variety of the "High" German (*Hochdeutsch* languages) as opposed to "Low" German (*Plattdeutsch*). But it is somewhat distinct from the High (Standard) German generally spoken in Germany today. There is a terminological problem because the "High" in High German can refer to both the mountainous origins of several German languages and also the language which has become the national literary and spoken language of Germany. I will refer to the latter as Standard German, although it is often known by the misleading term "High German." Both Deitsch and Standard German derive from High German dialects spoken in parts of German-speaking Central Europe, including the Rhine Valley and Switzerland, where the landscape is more mountainous than in northern Germany, the home of the Low German dialects. Standard German began to emerge in the sixteenth century from a group of eastern-central High German dialects, including the one employed by Martin Luther for his translation of the Bible. Modern Standard German thus developed in parallel to Pennsylvania Dutch, both varieties being descended from related but separate older dialects from the High German region. Pennsylvania German speakers who have traveled to the southwestern part of Germany

tell me that they can communicate with speakers of the regional dialects there, but have a difficult time understanding the Standard German spoken in cities such as Berlin or Hamburg.[8]

Although, as noted above, the "High" in "High German" is a geographic designation, many people, both in Germany and the United States, use "High German" to refer to the national language of Germany, and think it has a superior or higher status as a language. This idea reflects a prejudice in favor of an official, literary language. But Deitsch should be recognized as a vibrant, legitimate language. Many Deitsch speakers claim that Deitsch is more "expressive," and this expressiveness is valued in the speeches given at versammlinge. In fact, there are often complaints that some Deitsch speakers and writers, who know both Standard German and Deitsch, use too much Standard "High" German, suggesting that they are letting too much of that language seep into their use of Deitsch, and that Deitsch speakers are proud of their language without influence from Standard German.

For the early immigrants of the eighteenth century, Deitsch was not a written or literary language. When reading and writing, Pennsylvania Germans used Standard German, which was printed in their Bibles and newspapers, used in their church services, and engraved on their tombstones. A large Standard German–language press developed in the towns settled by the Pennsylvania Germans, including Philadelphia, Allentown, Reading, Ephrata, Lancaster, Harrisburg, and York. The use of Standard German eroded over the course of the nineteenth century, and by the end of the century, almost all literate Pennsylvania Germans used English as their main written language. The advent of World War I led to the final demise of most of the remaining Standard German literary journals. In the middle of the nineteenth century, some Pennsylvania Germans began experimenting with writing in their Deitsch "dialect" (there were similar regional dialect literatures developing in Europe). By 1900, there were books of poems, newspaper columns, and even plays written in Deitsch, and the literary tradition flourished through the middle of the twentieth century. Although not as strong at present, the tradition still continues. It has been strongly influenced by broader trends in American literature, especially the regional "local color" literature that was popular throughout

the nation in the late nineteenth and early twentieth centuries. Deitsch literature includes humorous and ethnic themes that are important in the versammlinge.[9]

There is a terminological debate over whether Pennsylvania German is a "language" or a "dialect." Many people in the region refer to Deitsch as "the dialect," and it is common to refer to works written in Deitsch as "dialect literature." Related languages and dialects can be analyzed by "lumping" or by "splitting": some scholars lump together related versions of a language into one, and others like to split them into separate languages. The point is that every language has regional and dialectical variations, and sometimes it is difficult to decide when those variations make it sensible to divide it into separate languages. Linguists often cite an adage, "a language is a dialect with an army and navy"; that is, the distinction between "language" and "dialect" is often based on politics and power, not any objective reality grounded in linguistics.[10] Pennsylvania Germans do not have their own army and navy, so perhaps they have a "dialect." In my view, however, they do have a distinctive language that derived from some dialects of the regions in and around southwest Germany, and then evolved into its present form in the United States, developing its own literature and distinctive contexts for use.

A further controversy arises from the orthographic and/or spelling conventions for Deitsch. Pennsylvania Germans began writing in Deitsch in the nineteenth century before there were any standardized spelling conventions for the language. Different authors used different spellings for the same word, and sometimes the same author spelled the same word in different ways. There are two basic approaches to spelling Deitsch words. One is based on the author's attempt to use American-English spelling equivalents to represent Deitsch words, and the other is based on Standard German spelling. Many Pennsylvania German writers do not know Standard German, but they all know English, and so many use Americanized spellings, with many individual variants. Writers with an academic or professional background often know Standard German and prefer a system based upon that knowledge. For the last fifty years, many scholars and the Pennsylvania German Society have preferred the Buffington-Barba-Beam system, based on Standard German and named

after the two Pennsylvania German scholars who originally developed it, Albert Buffington and Preston Barba, as well as C. Richard Beam, who has done extensive work in the language more recently.[11] Their argument is that since Pennsylvania German is related to Standard German, German spelling conventions are far more appropriate to represent it. However, many Pennsylvania Germans who are fluent speakers of Deitsch have difficulty reading the language, especially in an orthography based on Standard German. In this book, I will keep whatever spelling is found in the original documents, although I will note some of the inconsistencies. Readers are forewarned that the same term may have several different spellings depending upon the user and source.[12] This issue is an immediate problem in the representation of the term *versammling*. Although this is the preferred Buffington-Barba-Beam spelling, it is most often written as *fersommling* in Deitsch materials. One reader of a draft of this book, who was very familiar with versammlinge, did not recognize the term *versammling* in the title. On the other hand, when I was asked to give a title for a talk at a regional historical society, the organizer questioned my proposal to use *fersommling*, claiming that in her region of Lebanon County the proper spelling is *versammling*. I have chosen to follow the precedent of other scholars who use *versammling* in their publications, although these same scholars often use *fersommling* in printed materials for the actual meetings.[13]

Making Tradition Across Time

Pennsylvania Germans were and continue to be influenced by a variety of sources and, like all other Americans, change over time as the result of continual changes in technology, economic patterns, media, and interactions with other Americans. Even changing understandings of what it means to be "Pennsylvania German" have an impact on how Pennsylvania Germans understand themselves and behave. Pennsylvania German lives were different in 1750 and 1800, in 1850 and 1900, in 1950 and 2000, and I expect they will be different in 2050.

The participants in the versammlinge have lived through dramatic changes in the economy, media, and culture. The versammling founders were born in the late 1800s in a largely farming economy with many

distinctive Pennsylvania German folk practices. Over the course of their lives, they saw the introduction of electricity, indoor plumbing, telephones, gasoline-powered machinery, and automobiles. They saw the expansion of new mass media, including films and radio. They participated in many of these changes, and they also experienced the erosion of their indigenous cultural practices and language. Many left the farms for other professions and employment in a developing industrial economy.

During my research in the late twentieth and early twenty-first centuries, I talked with people who were born in the 1920s and '30s and also experienced dramatic changes. This group lived through the change from an agricultural economy to an industrial one and more recently the development of a postindustrial service economy. They experienced changes in media with the growth of radio and film, and then the introduction of television, cable programming, the Internet, and cell phones. Most, however, have strong memories of a rural upbringing, even though few still make a living through farming. In interviews, many recall times when people congregated at small businesses, general stores, communal harvesting, church events, picnics, and taverns to interact and talk, often remembering the conversations as being in Deitsch, and in fact many tell me these settings are where they learned Deitsch. To be sure, Pennsylvania Germans used and continue to use the new media and technologies to express themselves in the Deitsch language, and the automobile allowed for a mobility which helped the versammlinge and other heritage events to thrive. There were popular Deitsch columns in newspapers, a few Deitsch books, a few popular radio shows, and more recently a few public access cable shows with Deitsch programming. One can find several Deitsch sites on the Internet, mostly constructed by the few younger people who not only have some familiarity with the language but also Internet skills. But the electronic media are overwhelmingly in English and are increasingly pervasive. Both the use of Deitsch and the occasions for its use are becoming rare, and the children and grandchildren of versammling participants rarely have any fluency in Deitsch. It is unusual to find any Church Pennsylvania Germans born after World War II who can speak Deitsch. These processes of loss and replacement are not unique to the Pennsylvania Germans. They are part of global processes by which external national and international

cultural practices, relationships, frames of reference, forms of media, and symbolic meanings replace local ones, a process that sociologist Andrew Giddens has aptly described as "disembedding." The versammlinge offer an important opportunity for the more "embedded" expression of personal interaction, local meanings, humor, and drama in a society that has become much more impersonal. And the versammlinge offer opportunities to use and hear the Deitsch language.[14]

The people who attend the versammlinge are in many respects not much different from the general American population. They drive cars, and most use computers and have cell phones. Their children and grandchildren are on Facebook. They are concerned about current events. Many proudly served in the military. Many belong to service clubs and organizations that serve the general community, including Rotary, Lions, volunteer fire companies, and historical organizations, and have many other interests shared with the much larger non–Pennsylvania German population. They are fluent speakers of English, which is their primary language, although some do have "Dutchy" accents and use regional terms and expressions. Most were raised in or close to a rural environment where Deitsch was frequently spoken and some traditional folk practices were still followed. They have a commitment to speaking their Deitsch language and participating in events, like the versammlinge, that celebrate their language and heritage and remind them of a past time which was more rural. At versammlinge, this past is often described as lacking modern conveniences and a certain sophistication, but also as having admirable values and qualities. They are proud of their heritage.

Writing about heritage raises some personal issues for me. Growing up in the 1950s, I was fairly close to a war fought against two foes, Germany and Japan, whose propaganda claimed a special heritage to justify conquest, oppression, and genocide. In the United States, ancestral societies such as the General Society of Mayflower Descendants and the Daughters of the American Revolution seemed to me to use heritage in a troubling manner that was exclusionary and suggested a privileged position for a few people based upon ancestry. Moreover, many academics viewed "heritage" events as superficial and inaccurate in their representation of culture and history. When I first started studying anthropology in the 1970s,

"heritage" was not a popular term, and most anthropologists treated it as a process of distorting history and culture in order to legitimate privilege and domination. Many anthropologists still feel the same way. But more recently academics have started to value "heritage" events, and there are books and journals devoted to its study. Heritage is now often seen as representing efforts to celebrate, if not preserve, distinctive cultural traditions as powerful forces of globalization level and assimilate many indigenous cultural traditions. Heritage events are often a source of pride and also an assertion of legitimacy in the face of prejudice. Many people around the world, including on Sikaiana, the Polynesian island where I did over three years of ethnographic research, develop special ceremonies to praise their culture and past. I view the versammlinge as reflecting this latter, more positive expression of heritage. It struck me that, like so many people around the world, Pennsylvania Germans struggle with issues of praising their past, even trying to maintain some of it, while still participating in a rapidly changing modern world. Pennsylvania German heritage events are also partly a response to the prejudices of other Americans who think of the Pennsylvania Germans as inferior "dumb Dutch," or have distorted and false stereotypes about them. The versammlinge are occasions when Pennsylvania Germans can celebrate and appreciate their heritage and their ancestors' accomplishments. They are, moreover, events in which the Pennsylvania Germans can assess the effects of modernization by comparing the past with the present.[15]

Academics often criticize heritage events for being staged and distorting the past. Perhaps I am biased through having been involved in many different heritage events; nevertheless, I think these criticisms often overlook many of the important meanings for participants in these events. Reconstructing an accurate past is problematic for anyone, including the most erudite academic. Academic historians often disagree about how to interpret and represent the past, and professional anthropologists are notorious for disagreeing about how to interpret both a culture's past and present. Criticisms of heritage events often overlook the fact that these events are not only about the past, but also need to be understood as part of the present and how the past is interpreted by that present. Whatever heritage events say about the past, they become meaningful expressions

of culture and identity in their development and performance in the present.[16]

Pennsylvania Germans have continually redefined themselves both as American and as different in their ethnic patterns. Since colonial times, Pennsylvania Germans have been sensitive about their culture, language, and relations with their English-speaking neighbors. As early as the middle of the eighteenth century, Ben Franklin notoriously referred to the Pennsylvania Germans as "Palatine boors" and sought to assimilate them into the commonwealth's dominant English culture and language by providing them with a subsidized system of "charity" schools. The Pennsylvania Germans, however, strongly resisted the plan, and it ended in failure. Franklin was also worried about their possible lack of loyalty to the British Crown, especially during the French and Indian War. In that war, however, the Pennsylvania Germans were solidly behind the British, and in the War of Independence they were more likely to support the Continental Army's cause than many of Pennsylvania's inhabitants of British ancestry, some of whom, including Franklin's son, strongly supported the Tories.[17]

Steven Nolt has argued that from the days of the early Republic to the Civil War, Pennsylvania Germans have tried to preserve their distinctive traditions and resisted efforts to assimilate into a national culture, and in doing so they considered themselves to be part of a very American cultural pattern of independence and local autonomy, a process that Nolt terms "ethnicization-as-Americanization."[18] I found that a similar pattern continued in the definition of a Pennsylvania German ethnic identity in the nineteenth and twentieth centuries, but I prefer to refer to this process as "ethnic and American." By the time of the Civil War, Pennsylvania Germans were clearly "American," having lived in the region for six to eight generations. They were also preserving and developing a regional culture, language, and heritage. What it means to be an "American" changes, and so does how Pennsylvania Germans defined their distinct ethnicity.

Pennsylvania Germans preserved their unique culture far longer and developed many more events to celebrate their heritage than other immigrants, including other German Americans. Russell Kazal, in tracing the expression of German American ethnic identity in Philadelphia

in the late nineteenth and twentieth centuries, found that generally German American organizations, *Vereinswesen*, declined after the late 1890s. Several factors crosscut, transcended, and limited the development of German American identity, including a general pull toward a broader consumer culture that transcended ethnic identity, alliances between working-class German Americans and working-class Italian and Irish Americans that often emphasized a Catholic religious orientation, and problems with German American identity created by World War I. Kazal found that generally after World War I, middle-class German Americans started identifying with old-stock European Americans based in a general northwest European identity that included people with Nordic and English ancestry.[19] This history of assimilation and loss is in striking contrast to Pennsylvania German ethnicity, heritage, and identity, which was developed and maintained throughout the nineteenth century and well into the twentieth century.

The versammling movement shows how the Pennsylvania Germans have redefined and recreated themselves, both out of pride in their own accomplishments and in response to the prejudices of other Americans. In the late 1920s and 1930s, outsiders became enthralled with the distinctiveness of Pennsylvania German culture, and the automobile made mass tourism possible from nearby large urban centers. Pennsylvania Germans themselves, both anxious to express themselves and energized by the interest of outsiders, developed a range of heritage events, including the versammlinge.

2.

Making Tradition

THE ORIGINS AND DEVELOPMENT OF THE VERSAMMLINGE

Tradition is about the past, but all traditions have a beginning, and in this sense they are invented and constructed. By the time I was seeing the versammlinge in the late twentieth century, they had been an important event for nearly seventy years, and, although they began as a new way to celebrate Pennsylvania German traditions, they had become a tradition themselves. The expression of Pennsylvania German ethnicity has a long history, in some respects going back to their initial settlements and resistance to efforts, such as Franklin's "charity" schools, to assimilate them more fully into the dominant Anglo-American culture. This maintenance of a distinctive regional culture continued throughout the nineteenth and into the early twentieth century even as Pennsylvania German lives were strongly affected by industrialization. At the same time, they developed new ways and events to express and celebrate their distinctive heritage and ethnicity. World War I dampened these expressions of ethnicity as prejudice against Germany and things German swept across the country. In the late 1920s, as if some kind of cultural pressure had built up, there

was a strong resurgence of Pennsylvania German pride and events to express that pride. The versammlinge began during this resurgence.

In a pamphlet describing the groundhog lodges, Richard Miller, an active participant in the versammlinge and a retired professor of German at Kutztown University, writes that the origin of the lodges was partly a reaction to the hostility many Americans felt toward the German language and culture after World War I: "The people were not only concerned about attacks on their German heritage, but also the threat to the Pennsylvania German culture, traditions and the dialect."[1] In an interview, Miller told me,

> Hatred for the German language spilled over to the Pennsylvania German culture. And this is why guys like Pumpernickel Bill and Brendle and the whole gang were concerned, you know, that this would have a devastating effect on the Pennsylvania German community, and they felt something should be done to help preserve and perpetuate this dialect; and they felt the Pennsylvania German Grundsow lodge would be an excellent vehicle to get the guys to come out and speak the language and help promote the culture. That was one of the reasons. And then the other, like I say, was to get the guys together and have a night out with the boys and tell stories, dialect stories, and give an opportunity for people who did not necessarily have contact every day in the dialect, but understood the dialect, to come out and enjoy. Boy, it went off like gangbusters.

Carl Snyder, at the time the leader of Lodge #1 and of the Grossdaadi Lodge (Grandfather Lodge), which coordinates lodge meetings and activities, told me, "I know that when my dad was in World War I, there was prejudice, quite a bit of prejudice. And that was one of the reasons that they discontinued speaking the dialect. And that is why they started the groundhog lodges, they were going to do something to perpetuate the dialect, because it was dying." Both Carl and Richard served in World War II and said that there was little if any prejudice toward Pennsylvania Germans during that war.[2]

In the late 1920s and '30s, the renewed attention to Pennsylvania Germans came from both inside and outside the region. There was a

growing national interest in regional American cultures and a variety of folk festivals and events to celebrate them. There was also increased interest, which was probably enhanced by the New Deal, in the accomplishments of ordinary Americans. Pennsylvania German crafts such as *Fraktur* and redware dating back to the eighteenth century were the subject of museum exhibitions in New York and Philadelphia, and wealthy collectors representing the leading industrial families of the nation, including the Fords, Rockefellers, and du Ponts, were collecting these artifacts. Pennsylvania Germans themselves expressed their excitement about their culture by organizing events and festivals to celebrate their heritage, including a series of special events that centered around the Deitsch language. There were plays written in Deitsch that became popular in the region and playwriting contests; there were liar contests in which Pennsylvania Germans competed to tell the biggest tall tale in Deitsch; and there were special church services in Deitsch. It was in this context that the versammlinge developed as the most widespread and popular of Pennsylvania German Deitsch-language events.[3]

The first general versammling was held in 1933, and the first groundhog lodge meeting was held in 1934. Within a very short period of time, Deitsch-language events became widely popular. Church groups, community groups, and family picnics were organized centering on Pennsylvania German–language events that followed a very similar format. Over the coming years, many of these gatherings became formalized into annual events. Eventually, seventeen additional groundhog lodges were formed, modeled on the first lodge. Many more general versammlinge were organized with formats similar to that of the groundhog lodges, but their activities were not specifically associated with the groundhog, and, unlike the groundhog lodges, most were open to both men and women.

The Beginnings

The idea for holding a Deitsch-language event seems to have been simmering in the late 1920s and early 1930s. John Woodruff was a professor at Susquehanna University, a founding member and president of the Snyder County Trust Company, and a two-term representative for Snyder County

in the Pennsylvania State Assembly. On January 13, 1933, he held an organizational meeting to plan a Deitsch-language event, a versammling, in Selinsgrove, Snyder County.⁴ The actual event was held on March 9, 1933. During this time in Pennsylvania German regions, all newspapers were published in English, but many had a regular column in Deitsch. The Deitsch-language columnist for the *Selinsgrove Times* wrote that a "historic" meeting was held for Pennsylvania Germans. He suggested that the motivation was at least partly the Great Depression: "Der purpose war der depression tsu ferschrecka" (the purpose was to scare away the Depression).⁵ An English-language newspaper account also suggests the economic context of the Depression, describing Woodruff at the meeting as "complimenting the Pennsylvania Germans on their stability; holding their heads high up in this financial crisis."⁶ The event was also held as a tribute to Thomas H. Harter, a newspaper publisher who wrote a very popular Deitsch column in the nineteenth century about a fictional character named Boonastiel that was turned into several books.⁷ Harter is probably still the most popular Deitsch writer, and his writings use humorous homespun philosophy to deliver a message, just as many versammling activities do. His writing style was heavily influenced by the local color and regional humor writers who were very popular throughout the nation in the late nineteenth century.⁸

The Selinsgrove meeting included food, songs, speeches, and presentations, everything spoken in Deitsch. There were 158 people in attendance, all male. Harter made a humorous presentation about Pennsylvania German humor, asserting that "Irish wit cuts, but . . . Pennsylvania German wit is not felt until the blood comes." A telegram was read that was written in Deitsch and claimed to be from Franklin Roosevelt. The president apologized for his absence due to national affairs. This mixture of national and local remains very common in present-day versammling events.⁹

A few days later in Allentown, on March 13, 1933, William Troxell held an organizational meeting for a groundhog lodge. A traditional Pennsylvania German *Taufschein* (baptism certificate) commemorates this meeting (see figure 12). Troxell wrote that the event had been in the planning stages "for several years." The first groundhog lodge meeting was held on February 2, 1934, attended by about three hundred people.¹⁰

Given the similarities in structure between the meetings and the network of contacts between many of the people involved in the versammlinge, it seems probable that there was some contact between Troxell and Woodruff. Troxell, however, is not included on the list of people attending the first Selinsgrove event that was published in the *Selinsgrove Times*. Russell Gilbert, who was beginning a career as a professor of German at Susquehanna College, was closely involved with Woodruff in organizing the Selinsgrove event. Gilbert was a graduate of Muhlenberg College in Allentown, where he almost certainly took courses from Harry Hess Reichard and Preston Barba, professors in the German Department who had Pennsylvania German backgrounds and became closely involved with the versammlinge and many other heritage activities (Barba was on the original board of Groundhog Lodge #1). Troxell was the speaker at the annual meeting of the Selinsgrove group in 1936.[11]

After these initial meetings, many other versammlinge were organized. Often, they were church picnics or community events that included a meeting in Deitsch with food, songs, speeches, and theatrical performances. There was a very early "Deitsch picnic" held in Grange, Jefferson County, Pennsylvania, on August 9, 1934. Don Yoder, an eminent authority on the Pennsylvania Germans, writes that, although it is outside of the regions normally associated with the Pennsylvania Germans, there were a large number of Deitsch speakers in this region, which is very near Punxsutawney, the home of the nationally famous groundhog. (There does not seem to have been a groundhog included in this event.) Yoder notes that this gathering was followed by another in 1935.[12] What relationship it had to the events in Selinsgrove and Allentown is not clear, but it does suggest that there was a broad base of appeal for Deitsch-language events in the early 1930s. A program from the Millersville University library archives shows that in 1937 there was an all-Deitsch language event, Der Airscht Pennsylfawnish Deitscher Picknick (the First Pennsylvania German Picnic), in the small town of Bowers in northeast Berks County. Held at Bowers Busch (Bowers Park) on June 5, the event was sponsored by the nearby Saint Paul's Church. From the program, it is clear that it followed the general pattern to be outlined in the next chapter, with songs, speeches, food, and other Deitsch events.

One of the most popular general versammlinge was organized in 1937 in Berks County. The Berks County Fersommling was clearly influenced by the groundhog lodge meeting in Allentown, having a similar structure and including many of the same leaders, although without the groundhog imagery and including both men and women. It has met annually to the present, and as of 2014 has the largest attendance of any versammling, including the groundhog lodges. Alvin Kemp, county superintendent of schools in Berks County and a popular speaker at Deitsch-language events, is listed in the versammling's first program as the *Formaischder* (*Vormeeschder*, leader).[13] He described its origins in an article written in early 1945: "The founding of the Berks County Versammling was first discussed in a motor car by a group on the way home from a meeting of the Allentown Grundsau [groundhog] Lodge, and every one of the passengers in that car is a member n[o]w of the Berks County Versammling Committee."[14]

In this article, Kemp identified twenty-five different annual versammling Deitsch-language events, which he divided into types: Versammlinge; Grundsow (groundhog); Church Versammlinge, Folk Festivals and Summer Versammlinge; and Picnicks [*sic*]. He does not list all the events being held; for example, he does include the Berks County Fersommling but not the ones discussed above in Grange or Bowers. Presumably there were so many that it was not possible to know about all of them. Kemp also identified the objectives of these meetings: a night of wholesome entertainment; a substantial Pennsylvania "Dutch" meal; familiarity with Pennsylvania German history and traditions; appreciation of Pennsylvania German folklore; a renewal of pride in the soul of the Pennsylvania Germans; curbing of unjust and undeserved criticism of writers and speakers; and revitalization of the Pennsylvania German language.[15] These objectives are still important seventy years later.

The Groundhog Lodges

Although the first versammling was held in Selinsgrove, William Troxell of Allentown was the key organizer of versammlinge throughout southeastern Pennsylvania. Under the nom de plume of "Pumpernickle Bill," Troxell wrote a Deitsch-language column for the *Allentown Morning Call*

and was active in many Pennsylvania German folk activities and presentations.[16] Troxell's organizational meeting in 1933 determined the pattern for the organization of the all other Deitsch groundhog lodges and most of the general versammlinge. Each group has an overseeing *Raad* or *Rawd*, which can be translated as "wheel"; it is also the Deitsch term for a church consistory, council, or board of directors. The leading officers of the *Raad* are the *Amtsleit* or *Ombtsleit*. They consist of a *Habtmon* or *Haaptmann* in the groundhog lodges, or *Formaischder, Formeschder, Vormeeschder* in other general versammlinge (leader or president); a *Schreiver* or *Schreiwer* (writer, i.e., secretary); a *Gelthaver* or *Gelthewer* (money holder, i.e., treasurer); and a *Fuder Maischder* or *Meeschder* (food master, i.e., menu supervisor). Some groups have added other offices, including an *Unner Haaptmann* (vice president) and *Fohrsinger* or *Vorsinger* (song leader). (For simplicity and to help non-Deitsch readers, I will use the English terms.) There are traditionally thirteen members of a groundhog lodge board. According to Troxell, this number was chosen "to show that we were not superstitious because we were going to honor the groundhog as a weather prophet," which I interpret as play on a continuing theme of the ironic tension between modern and traditional. The organizers wanted to show their allegiance to premodern, nonscientific beliefs, at the same time that they constantly winked about their true commitment to those beliefs (see figures 2, 17, and 22 for pictures of the board).[17]

Non-groundhog general versammlinge have similar officers, although they do not have the rule about thirteen board members. As board members retire or pass away, members of the board select replacements, who are then approved at the annual versammling by all those attending. The board usually meets several times a year to organize the annual meeting. Tickets are sold to the annual meetings. In past years, meetings were full and it was difficult, even impossible, to get tickets. Tickets were often passed down in family lines. By the late 1990s, when I started this study, it was much easier to get tickets. Attendance has fallen as older people have died, and there are fewer and fewer people who can speak Deitsch (see figures 10 and 11).

The groundhog legend is based upon a European belief that hibernating animals, such as bears and badgers, come out in midwinter to examine their shadows. If the sun is shining and the animals see their shadows,

then there is going to be a longer winter. This legend was transferred to the groundhog when the ancestors of the Pennsylvania Germans arrived in America. Troxell's personal papers show that he had contact with other groups that were celebrating Groundhog Day, including one at Quarryville in southern Lancaster County, Pennsylvania, and the very famous one in Punxsutawney, Pennsylvania, although these groups did not have any emphasis on Pennsylvania German heritage and language.[18]

Alfred Shoemaker, a towering scholar in Pennsylvania German studies, did extensive archival and newspaper research into all aspects of Pennsylvania German culture.[19] His notes, which can be found at Myrin Library, Ursinus College, show that the groundhog legend was well known in the Pennsylvania region in the nineteenth century. February 2 is also the Christian holiday of Candlemas, when church candles are blessed for the coming year. The holiday marks the day when, following Jewish tradition, Mary took Jesus to the synagogue forty days after his birth. This day also had practical significance for Pennsylvania German farmers. It marked the midpoint between winter and spring, at least by the solstices, and therefore farmers calculated that they had to have half their winter fodder still saved. During the winter months, women spent a lot of time spinning, but by early February it was time to turn to other chores, and there were more hours of sunlight, extending daylight until the evening meal. Shoemaker's notes include variations of a common Pennsylvania German saying:

Lichtmess
Schpinna fergess
Bauer halb fuuder fress
Un bei dawg tsu nacht ess.

Preston Barba, in his popular 'S Pennsylfawnisch Deitsch Eck column in the *Allentown Morning Call*, records a similar saying:

Lichtmess	[Candlemas
Schpinne vergess;	Stop [forget] spinning
Bei Daag zu Nacht gess',	It is light at the evening meal
Un's halb Fudder gfiediert.	Half the fodder has been eaten.][20]

SERIOUS NONSENSE

In his book about Groundhog Day, Don Yoder suggests that the origins of Candlemas and Groundhog Day go even deeper than Christian times to Celtic practices that took place on four days concerned with seasonal change: November 1, February 1, May 1, and August 1. This concern with seasonal changes, so important to people who live by farming, became the basis for the celebration of a special day at the beginning of February.[21]

Ellwood D. Fisher, a Deitsch column writer for the *Allentown Morning Call* in the early twentieth century, refers to the groundhog legend in a column from February 17, 1902. His passage shows that the legend was well known and demonstrates the brand of humor in which outside sophisticates and moderns are ridiculed, which still continues in versammling humor more than a hundred years later.

Gell, ich hob der's g'sawt der dox[22] wehs eppes? Der wedder-mocher in Washington secht wull er deht net, awwer seller is yuscht jealous, sell is oll. Mihr wuh unser wedder schun hunnerta fun yohra mocha hen lussa fun der grundsow luss'n uns mohl of course net obschrecka fun so'ma dinda schlecker in Washington un geh'n tzurrick uff unser olter freund. Oh nay! Un wos wissa sie don in Washington fum wedder ennyhow? Sie gev'ns olla dag rous awwer worta bis's doh is, un won's tzudreft is's gute un won net is's yuscht ferfehlt, un'r grickt sei geld olla mohnat, un schoft uff der principle "net g'schussa is aw ferfehlt," un won mihr mohl eh dag sawga missa well'm os mer's g'schwinscht glauva, der grundsow udder sell'm wedder mon dert in

[*Yes, didn't I tell you that the groundhog knows something? The weather-maker in Washington denies it, but he is only jealous, that's all. We who have had our weather made already for hundreds of years by the groundhog will not be frightened by such an ink-licker*[23] *in Washington, nor will we turn our back on an old friend. Oh, no! What does he* [*in Washington*] *know about weather anyhow? He forecasts it daily but waits until it has arrived; when accurate it is well, and if inaccurate it is just a miss. He gets his pay each month and operates on the principle "no shot is a miss." Should we some day be obliged to say whom we'd believe soonest, the groundhog or the fellow there in Washington, you would find us unanimous in favor*

Washington, don werscht duh finna os mer oll ehschtimmich sawga der grundsow, un shem'n uns aw net's tzu sawga. *of the groundhog, and wouldn't be ashamed to say it.*]24

The original charter of Groundhog Lodge #1 explains the organization's existence, stating in English:25

> Whereas, There is at present a wide spread tendency to deride and ridicule the common woodchuck, commonly called "Grundsow" as a weather prophet, and a creature of truth, foresight and integrity, and
>
> Whereas, We who have known the groundhog from childhood on, have found him an honorable and reliable creature and our best long distance weather prophet,
>
> Therefore, We the undersigned have bound ourselves together for the purpose of defending his reputation, and honoring his insight into the future, and have for this purpose adopted the following constitution.

This use of highly formal, officious speech recurs throughout the meetings and is another example of what I find to be an undercurrent of irony in the events.

My own experience with people in the region is that, despite its symbolic importance in Pennsylvania German identity at lodge meetings, groundhogs are not admired in daily life. Groundhogs are pests. They eat garden crops, and they dig holes that can be hazardous for larger farm animals, such as horses and cattle. In past times, however, farming families made them into a meal. Many people who were brought up on farms or in rural surroundings still remember eating groundhog, and they tell me that, if prepared in the right way, it can be a good meal. But it is rarely, if ever, eaten at present.

Regardless of these practical concerns, the idea of a special ceremony for the groundhog took off, and other groundhog lodges were founded. The following is a list of groundhog lodges, their location, and the year they were established.

Lodge #1 on da Lechaw 1934, Allentown, Lehigh County
Lodge #2 on da Skippach 1938, Souderton, Montgomery County
Lodge #3, Filadelfy 1938, Temple University, Philadelphia
Lodge #4, on da Dohek 1949, Quakertown, Bucks County
Lodge #5 on da Schwador im Bind Busch 1948, Pine Grove, Schuylkill County
Lodge #6 on Pokopoho 1951, McIlhaney, Towamensing, Stroudsburg, Monroe and Carbon Counties
Lodsch #7 G'shwishich da Barioma un da Magowi 1952, East Greenville, Montgomery County
Lodge #8 on da Lizzard Grick 1954, New Ringgold, Schuylkill County
Lodge #9 on da Deef Runn 1955, Dublin, Bucks County
Lodge #10 on da Braidkeppicha Grick 1956, Brodheadsville, Monroe County
Lodge #11 on da Feierling 1957, Fireline, Carbon County
Lodge #12 on da Dulpehockae Pawd 1960, Tulpehocken, Shartlesville, Berks County
Lodge #13 on da Insche Grick 1963, Emmaus, Lehigh County
Lodge #14 on da Saakna Grick 1963, Coopersburg, Lehigh County
Lodge #15 fon Barricks Koundi 1967, Kutztown, Berks County
Lodge #16 om Jahden 1972, Orefield, Lehigh County
Lodge #17 om Union Kanal 1982, Myerstown, Lebanon County
Lodge #18 on da Gross Forelle Grick 1992, Emerald, Lehigh County

The activities of the lodges are followed by articles in regional newspapers, which often tie them into the general public interest in Groundhog Day. For many years, the *Allentown Morning Call* often included prominent announcements about lodge activities, especially those of Lodge #1, which held most of its meetings in Allentown. Every year from 1935 through the 1970s, the *Morning Call* ran an announcement of the lodge's coming activities. With some minor changes in wording, the announcement read:

> Grundsow Lodge Proclamation
> Be It known that E. J. Balliet, by the authority in me vested as habtmon of the Grundsow Lodge Nummer Ains an da Lechaw do hereby

proclaim that Groundhog Day, the second day of February 1935, shall be observed in manner as follows:

First: Each and every member shall early in the morning face to the east and make careful observations of the color of the sunrise, cloudiness of the sky, velocity and direction of the winds and general visibility.

Second: That each and every member shall repair to some well-known haunt, there after giving the high sign of the order, to observe and note all signs and sounds between the hours of 11:30 AM and 12:30 PM according to the secret instructions received in the closed lodge.

Third: No person shall disclose to any other person the nature of his observations but shall meditate deeply and seriously upon them until the convening of the lodge on Monday evening at 7 O'clock, February 4, 1935 in the Masonic Temple, Allentown, where and when all findings have been duly considered and weighed, the official prognostication will be announced.

Done this first day of February, 1935, A.D.

E. J. Balliet

Habtmon, Grundsow Lodge Nummer Ains an da Lechaw

Attest:

"Pumpernickel Bill" Troxell, Schreiver[26]

An editorial praising the celebration of Groundhog Day appeared in the *Morning Call* on February 3, 1941, commenting, "It is good that all this is so for, in times like these especially, people welcome anything that temporarily at least takes their minds away from the stark facts of a greatly distressed world that appears to be moving toward greater and greater troubles and woes."[27]

In 1971, an editorial in the *Morning Call* blasted the *New York Times* for printing an article criticizing the widespread activities and obsessions surrounding Groundhog Day. The *Morning Call*'s editors made a stout defense of the Pennsylvania German groundhog: "Frankly we suspect that the only reason that the New York Times calls the Groundhog Day tradition a myth is because they can't communicate with the grundsow. He still speaks only

in Pennsylvania Dutch and shows no inclination to change this custom to satisfy any doubting editors."[28]

In recent years, the *Morning Call* has continued to cover the activities of Lodge #1, although with less prominence, partly due, perhaps, to the newspaper's having changed ownership in the 1980s from a local family to a national corporation. Moreover, the Pennsylvania German population is less visible in the region as the presence of other ethnic groups, notably Latinos, has grown with their population.[29]

Thus far, only one of the eighteen widely recognized groundhog lodges has disbanded. Lodge #3, which was located in North Philadelphia at Temple University, was formed in 1938 and continued to have meetings until at least 1968 and perhaps even later. In a letter to Leonard Shupp written in 1992, ninety-three-year-old Millard Gladfelter, a retired administrator at Temple University, described the origins of the lodge: "I was invited to the Allentown (Lehigh) Grundsow Lodge. It was so enjoyable and impressive that many months later a few Dutchmen and I who were then at Temple University invited Troxell and Brendle to lunch at the faculty club. They were two interesting and solid persons. We resolved to take a try at a meeting of Grundsows at Temple. . . . Our Philadelphia attendance rose to 300 in years. But mobility of population and pressure for survival seem more paramount to urbanites these days than celebrating the folklore and memories of our heritage. That's good and bad."[30]

There are at least two lodges that are somewhat outside the mainstream. In Delaware, where many Pennsylvania educators had moved to teach, a "groundhog lodge" met on the campus of the University of Delaware and later in Newark from 1950 until 1978. The Delaware lodge often invited well-known Pennsylvania Germans as speakers, including the Reverend Clarence Rahn. This lodge is not widely known among present-day lodge members, but David Geissinger, its last leader, told me that it was less structured in its activities than the other versammlinge, with widespread use of English and the inclusion of women at meetings (unusual for a groundhog lodge).

A women's (*Weibsleit*) groundhog lodge was started in 1985 in East Greenville, about forty-five miles north of Philadelphia. In theory, only women are invited to attend, although there are men involved as speakers,

servers, and guests. Like the Delaware lodge, the women's lodge has a looser formation and a much wider use of English than other groundhog lodges. The women's lodge is not centered on protesting the male exclusivity of the groundhog lodges, and there is a lot of cooperation with leading participants in the male lodges. The women's lodge's meetings do not include much groundhog ceremonialism and strike me as similar to the general versammlinge. The lodge's organizer, Lucy Kern, emphasized to me that it was developed to provide women a chance to get together. She is especially concerned that older women, many widowed, do not have enough opportunities to socialize.[31]

In 1987, the groundhog lodges came together to form the Grossdaadi Lodge (Grandfather Lodge), which oversees and coordinates the activities of all the lodges.[32] The Grossdaadi Lodge meets every fall, and most of the lodges send representatives. The lodge sponsors classes in the Deitsch language. Usually, these are weekly classes for adults run by lodge members. Many people who attend these and other similar Deitsch-language schools sponsored by other organizations are Deitsch "overhearers," a term used by Jennifer Schlegel to describe people who heard the Deitsch language from parents or grandparents as youngsters, although they never achieved much fluency in the language themselves.[33] The number of classes varies, depending upon the availability of instructors. In 2013, there were six different classes, which were held in churches or community centers. The teachers are volunteers and usually have no formal training in teaching or linguistics. Over four thousand diplomas were awarded to people who attended these classes between 2001 and 2011.[34]

The Grossdaadi Lodge also sponsored the development of a Pennsylvania German flag. Carl Snyder, who was the leader of both Lodge #1 and the Grossdaadi Lodge, explained to me that all the other ethnic groups in Allentown had their own flags, and he felt the Pennsylvania Germans should have one of their own as well. The flag includes four designs to represent four important aspects of Pennsylvania German life: the tulip to represent their artistic achievement; the Conestoga wagon to represent their manufacturing achievement; the plow to represent their farm life; and a church to represent the importance of religion and religious freedom. The center of the flag includes a picture of the ship that

brought the first Pennsylvania German ancestors to Pennsylvania in 1683, and around the ship are the words "Liewer Gott in himmel drin, Loss uns Deitsche was mir sin" (Dear God in heaven, let us Deitsche [Pennsylvania Germans] be what we are), from a saying that is a prominent part of every versammling (see figure 13).[35]

The Loss of Deitsch

Attendance at all the versammlinge has fallen. Lodge #1 attracted over 800 participants in the 1980s, but by 2013 attendance was down to about 225; the Berks County Fersommling has fallen from about 1000 in 2001 to below 500 in 2014. As older generations pass on, fewer of their children can speak Deitsch. It can be hard to find new board members. Although only one well-known groundhog lodge, the one at Temple University, has been discontinued (the lodge in Delaware was also discontinued, but it was not widely known and its inclusion of English and women took it out of the mainstream), numerous general versammlinge have been disbanded. Most people recognize that the future for most of the versammlinge is limited. Some expect an evolution to the greater inclusion of English, which is already happening in some of the lodges. Others, who are purists, do not feel that the English language can express Pennsylvania German experiences as well, and are not interested in events that include English. As of this writing in 2015, there are still seventeen active groundhog lodges and about twenty active general versammlinge.[36]

The loss of Deitsch speakers came about for many reasons. School policies in the late nineteenth century emphasized the use of English, and by 1900 leading Pennsylvania German educators strongly supported the exclusive use of English in schools. Clyde Stine, who studied the use of Deitsch in schools as part of his doctoral dissertation at Cornell University and became a very popular versammling speaker, found that there was a very hostile policy toward Deitsch in schools even among Pennsylvania German educators.[37] Many people told me that their parents were determined to teach them English before they started school so they would not go through the embarrassment that their parents had faced for not knowing English. There was also pressure to learn English in order to be

successful in the broader society. Many people felt that a "Dutchy" accent was a stigma that limited success. Finally, the rural life that supported Deitsch was eroded, especially after World War II. Non-Deitsch people were moving into the region, many participants in the versammlinge married spouses who did not speak Deitsch, and all the various forms of mass media, almost exclusively in English, were permeating and replacing the Deitsch that had been spoken on street corners, in shops, and in taverns.

In a detailed study of changing patterns of language use across four generations of Pennsylvania Germans, Achim Kopp found that there were still a large number of older Deitsch speakers in his study region, the Mahantongo Valley, about forty miles north of Harrisburg. Kopp separated the Deitsch speakers in his study into two groups: an Old Order Anabaptist group, which he labeled "sectarians," and another group which he labeled "nonsectarians" (mostly Church Pennsylvania Germans). The Anabaptists retained the Deitsch language across several generations. Among the nonsectarian (Church) people, there were a large number of elderly Deitsch speakers, but across generations the language was being lost. Most of their grandchildren had minimal, if any, ability to speak the language. Kopp traces the erosion of Deitsch among the nonsectarian groups to the loss of close community ties and networks which came about as a result of modernization and mobility. In contrast, the sectarians maintain their close networks and also keep the Deitsch language. Kopp found that there are a few contexts in which the nonsectarian people describe themselves as still using the Deitsch language, including at senior centers, while hunting with friends, and at the annual versammling in Lykens, a nearby town. Many in the older generation of nonsectarian speakers spoke English with a distinctive "Dutchy" accent, which their grandchildren had mostly lost. Kopp's study was done in 1989 and 1990, and another generation has passed with the loss of many more Deitsch speakers.[38]

Kopp's research demonstrates the dynamics at work that lead to the replacement of Deitsch by English. Most of his conclusions correspond with my own general experiences in the region, although I find younger people ambivalent about the Deitsch language and culture, sometimes making fun of their "Dutchy" elders for their accents and some of their old-fashioned ways, while also regretting the loss of the language and culture.

Many languages throughout the world are facing loss, even extinction, as the result of globalization, modernization, and contact between the dominant languages of powerful groups and the minority languages of the less powerful. I saw patterns of language loss on Sikaiana in the Solomon Islands, in which young people spoke Pijin (a language that mixed English and indigenous languages and developed to communicate across different indigenous languages) and English, although language loss there was not as severe as Deitsch for the Church people.[39] Some predict that half of the world's six to seven thousand languages will be lost by 2100. Within this pattern of global change, there are quite variable patterns of language shift, replacement, and loss. Deitsch will not be lost, at least not for quite a while, because of the large number of Old Order speakers. The number of speakers among Church people, however, who once constituted the great majority of its speakers, is rapidly dwindling. Often, as a language erodes and loses speakers, the ancestral language is preserved only in special or ceremonial contexts, a process that seems to be taking place among the Pennsylvania Germans. A study of the use of Yiddish by elderly Jewish Americans in Philadelphia found that most of their children have not learned the language. These elderly Jews treasure trips to a senior center, where they can continue to use the language. A study of the Kaska of the Yukon, in Canada, found that elders are the sources for the knowledge and use of the Kaska language. Younger Kaska people have come to associate the language with a kind of traditionalism and respect for the elderly that inhibits the language's preservation across generations.[40] As in these cases, Deitsch is preserved by elders in special domains, like versammlinge, while it is lost among younger people.

Participation

Contemporary social theory is concerned with issues of stratification and social class. Whenever I speak to an academic audience, I am asked about the social class of the versammling participants. Among those speaking Deitsch, participation in versammlinge cuts across social and economic backgrounds, both in the past and at present. The composition of the versammling boards and audiences includes a wide swath across different

backgrounds, including professionals, teachers, pastors, small business people, laborers, and farmers. Politicians, including occasionally members of the U.S. Congress, have attended the meetings (and still do). One present-day well-known speaker told me that he was very impressed as a youngster in the 1950s when he attended his first meeting and found so many civic, educational, and business leaders there. The real initiative for developing the lodges seems to have come from a professional middle class of educators, preachers, farmers, and small business people who wanted to recall their Pennsylvania German upbringing. College professors have been involved, notably Woodruff and Gilbert of Susquehanna University at the first Selinsgrove meeting, Preston Barba of Muhlenberg College, who was among the founders of Lodge #1, and many others over the years. A larger role is played and continues to be played by educators in primary and secondary education, such as Alvin Kemp, who was superintendent of Berks County schools. Pastors also play a very prominent role as board members and speakers. Many of the founders and leaders came from modest, often humble, rural backgrounds, and the events offered a way to connect with these roots. The content of the versammlinge recalls earlier times in small-town rural life, when social distinctions were not so clear. Because of language loss, there are far fewer speakers now. The language was retained longer in rural families than in professional ones, and so the current membership includes many people with rural roots, although most no longer work full-time on farms. The only real requirement for attendance is that one pay about twenty dollars for the dinner and know enough Deitsch to enjoy oneself. The board members and officers are selected because of their interest in the language and Pennsylvania German heritage and their willingness to devote time to organizing activities. Many of the leaders and active members, whether they are college educated or not, are involved in a variety of different service clubs, church organizations, several different versammlinge, local historical societies, and other heritage events.

The main organizers of most versammlinge, both the groundhog lodges and the general versammlinge, were male. Most of the speakers for all versammlinge were and continue to be male. The first versammling in Selinsgrove was all male; the versammling in Lykens is all male, voted in 1990 to stay that way, and remains so to this day.[41] There are several

versammlinge that are all female, including the female groundhog lodge in East Greenville. The larger participation of males resulted from a variety of factors. Males played a more prominent role in all phases of public life for much of the twentieth century and had a more prominent role in all heritage events and in academia than women. Some of the humor has sexual overtones, which were considered inappropriate for mixed company for much of the twentieth century, and these social conventions continue to influence many of the participants in the versammlinge, who are now in their seventies, eighties, and nineties.

Many of the founders of the versammling movement were members of fraternal organizations, notably the Freemasons, and important activities at groundhog lodges are directly derived, although usually with a humorous twist, from Masonic practices. Masons are still prominent members of many lodges. Fraternal organizations were central institutions in the social fabric of small towns in this region from the late nineteenth century into the middle of the twentieth century. I learned about their importance from experience. I had originally moved to the Pennsylvania German region to study the intensity of interpersonal relations in small towns. In learning about the region, I found that there were a variety of institutions that created social cooperation and solidarity: civic organizations, public administrative institutions (including schools, school boards, and school-affiliated groups), service clubs, historical societies, fire companies, and many others. Although relations there were not as tightly woven as on the little Polynesian island where I lived for several years, there seemed to be far more solidarity in these towns than in the relatively impersonal and commercial organizations of my upbringing in the suburbs of Philadelphia. I was also surprised to find that for many years, from the late 1800s until about World War II, there were very active groups of fraternal organizations in this region. The Freemasons, the Oddfellows, the Patriotic Order Sons of America, and the Grange, among many others, were important institutions in these towns. Unfortunately, there is surprisingly little scholarship on or recognition of the importance of these groups.[42]

The few academic studies of fraternal organizations have found that they united men of different class and social backgrounds during a period

of change. They were a male domain in an industrializing world that was becoming increasingly fragmented as households, factories, and businesses became separate domains, with the household associated with the feminine and the economic locations associated with emerging class differences. The fraternal lodge events included highly ritualized activities that both created fraternal bonding and encouraged self-development as members worked their way through different levels of lodge achievement. In a study of the fraternal lodges, Mary Ann Clawson summarizes: "[Masonic lodges] thus offered the vision of a society in which individual advancement and social solidarity were complementary rather than antagonistic—and attempted to create that society in miniature."[43] Moreover, the fraternal organizations flourished in a time before television, cable programming, or the Internet, providing opportunities for face-to-face interaction, fellowship, and amusement.

Although Freemasons were and remain important in the versammling activities, people who are not members of fraternal organizations are welcomed at all versammlinge, including the groundhog lodges, and often have important roles. Knowledge of Deitsch creates an egalitarianism that accepts all who understand and appreciate the Deitsch language, regardless of background, and the emphasis on fellowship is important to all types of versammlinge. Pennsylvania Germans talk with pride about others from outside the region and without Pennsylvania German ancestry who learned to speak Deitsch, including communities of African Americans who worked with Pennsylvania Germans, some Yiddish speakers who picked up the language, and immigrants to the region who lived with Pennsylvania German families. Somewhat like the fraternal organizations, the versammlinge create an opportunity for fellowship in a modernizing, differentiating society, and also a chance to use the Deitsch language, which was widely spoken before much of the modernization and differentiation took place.

The versammlinge are primarily for those who understand the language, and in fact at this point exclude many people with Pennsylvania German ancestry, including most of the spouses, children, and grandchildren of the participants. Much of the ethnic humor is the Pennsylvania Germans laughing at themselves. It ridicules those, no matter their

ancestry, who claim a special sophistication and superiority, a theme that is derived from widespread comic traditions in American humor.

Participants in the lodge share a commitment to their Pennsylvania German heritage. They like the opportunity to hear the Deitsch language, which is rarely spoken in their daily lives. The language is often described as more colorful than English. It also takes them to the times of their youth, when Deitsch was commonly spoken and was the language of family members who have since passed on.[44] They also enjoy the fellowship of being with others from a range of backgrounds who share in the language and events. When I asked Carl Snyder, an important and active leader, what was most important about the meetings, he replied, "The fraternal relationship that you have with the guys. Speaking the dialect, telling stories, good ethnic food, night out with the fellows, and you knew that you were preserving the language."

3.

"Let Us *Deitsche* Be What We Are"

THE STRUCTURE OF VERSAMMLING EVENTS

⟶

Although each versammling has some unique features and there have been some modifications over the years, the basic format of all versammlinge has remained very similar for over eighty years. The format includes a prayer, the Pledge of Allegiance to the American flag, a meal, songs, some kind of theatrical entertainment, and a speech that should include some humor and a message or, as participants say, a "text." The specific content within this format changes and often addresses contemporary issues as current events, politics, and popular culture all find their way into the skits, humor, and speeches. The format allows for performative opportunities to preserve and express personal face-to-face interactions and add to the tension between a simpler but naïve past and a highly technological but perplexing present. The content is constantly new and fresh, while the overall format remains constant, traditional, and ritualized. The medium itself compounds the contrasts between past and present.

I had attended many versammling meetings and talked with many people who were involved in the meetings in a variety of different ways,

but I never appreciated the amount of work that goes into preparing a meeting before I became involved with the preparations for meetings of Lodge #1. The officers hold quarterly meetings and then several other meetings as the date of the event comes closer. They have to find a place to hold the versammling, work out a menu, put together a program, find speakers for different activities, hire musicians, prepare a skit, send out invitations, and mail tickets to those who respond. The meeting room itself has to be decorated and prepared for the meeting. Some lodges have other events that accompany a meeting; for example, several lodges have special outdoor events at sunrise on the morning of February 2 (see figure 35). Although the same meeting places, menus, decorations, and bands are often used for several years in row, there is still a lot of work and preparation. The board members use the previous year's format to prepare for the coming year. And there are efforts to maintain tradition by keeping the same order of events from the ringing of the bell at the beginning to the parting words at the end.

The most important aspect of the versammlinge is the use of the Deitsch language in all activities (see figure 14). At the early meetings, people had to enter through an imitation groundhog hole made of straw. William Troxell described admission to the lodge: "In the early years a sign was placed above the entrance door, 'Check your hats and coats there' (an arrow pointing to the checkroom) and continuing the sign said, 'fom loch ob wert Deitsch g'shwetzt,' (from the hole on, only Dutch will be spoken)."[1] Almost all the speeches and presentations from the podium are done in Deitsch, and in theory, any use of English results in a fine. At the versammlinge I have attended, the rare presentations or short statements in English from the podium are usually made after a dramatic placement of money into a cup. Among the audience, the paying of fines is sporadic, though there may have been more rigorous monitoring in the past. The fines are collected at the end of each meeting and given to a local charity. Use of English has been increasing in recent years, and some versammlinge have incorporated more English into their events and become less strict about fines. It is also becoming increasingly difficult to find Deitsch-speaking performers and speakers.

The Structure of Meetings

The following discussion is based primarily upon the activities of the meetings of Groundhog Lodge #1. This lodge, which held its first full meeting in 1934, has the longest record of meetings and was the source of the development of other groundhog lodges and the versammling movement more generally. The basic structure of the meeting is similar for all versammlinge, although the groundhog lodges have a special emphasis on the activities of the groundhog. Two programs for Lodge #1 are given here, one from the first meeting in 1934, and another from the seventy-eighth meeting in 2014 (the lodge did not meet for three years during World War II because the members did not want to have fun while so many others were serving the country). The discussion follows the important events listed in these programs, most of which take place in all versammlinge. Headings list the events in English, followed by the event in Deitsch; the spellings have been left as in the originals.

Bringing in the Groundhog

Although not listed in the programs, the meetings at Lodge #1 begin with a ceremony that brings in the groundhog. The leader rings a bell, lights are lowered, the band plays rousing music, and men in top hats carry a stuffed groundhog inside a case. The groundhog is placed at the front of the meeting hall directly under the speaker's podium along with two other stuffed groundhogs (see figures 15, 21).

Singing "America"

Lied "America" in the 1934 program; *Lied—Amerika* in the 2014 program

After the groundhog is brought in at the beginning of the meetings, the gathering sings "America" ("My Country, 'Tis of Thee") in Deitsch. An example of the wording can be found in the 2014 program (*Mei Land, ich sing fun dir . . .*). The song shows both patriotism and, by being sung in Deitsch, loyalty to Pennsylvania German heritage.

Pledge of Allegiance to the Flag

Ferschpreches tzum Fahne in the 2014 program

The Pledge of Allegiance first appears in the 1982 program, as the second activity after singing "America," but it was very likely part of early meetings.

DIE SHPRECH ORDNUNG

Lied—"America" .... Die Fersomm'ld Lodge
        Der Dr. Harold Marcks fon Allentown, is der fohrsinger.
Gebet
Ferbinnerrei .... Habtmon Balliet
Owet Essa
Musick .... 'M Fenstermacher sei Deitchie Band
Ouslaiging .... Beim Habtmon
Lied—"Die Groundsow" .... Die Fersomm'ld Lodge
Der Regel Fohrlaisa .... Beim Schreiver
Der Regel Aw nemma .... Beim Habtmon
Die Wedder oussicht .... Elmer Fehnel un Mark Hoffman
Musick .... Die Band
Shtick—" 'S, A B C" .... Roy Brunner
Lied—"O Adoline" .... Die Fersomm'ld Lodge
Rade—"Hinner Grund fon da Penna. Deitcha" .... Dr. Edwin Fogel
Shticker—G'schriva un gewwa beim .... Ralph Funk
Die Ombtsleit Om Grunsow Loch .... beim T. R. Brendel
                          Die Shpieler
Thomas Brendel   Harvey Hankee   Julius Lentz
Pumpernickle Bill   Charles Oswald   Samuel Brader
Shtick—"Fartsich Yohr Tzurick" .... Ralph Sotzing
'S Shpin Lied .... Edmund Peters un Thomas Hoffman
Rade .... Pumpernickle Bill
Lied—"Die Boll Melinda" .... Die Fersomm'ld Lodge
Shtick—"Der G'wandel Tae" .... g'schrive un gewwa beim John Birmelin
Rade .... Thomas R. Brendel
Die Schnitzelbonk in Penna. Deitch. g'schriva un galead beim .... John Birmelin

1934 Program from Groundhog Lodge #1.

Die Shprech Ordnung

Lied – Amerika .... Die Fersomme'ld Lodge
Fohrsinger: Die Rhinelanders

Mei Land, ich sing fun dir,
Siess is die Freiheet mir,
Do will ich sei;
So wie die alde leit,
So fiel ich aw noch heit,
Sin dir zu yedre zeit
Immer gedrei.

Unsrer for-eldre Gott,
Fiehr uns in yedre not
An Deinre hand;
So lang mir dir gedrei,
Bleibt des Land gros un frei,
Du sollscht uns Keenich sei,
Schutz unserm Land.

  -John Birmelin

Ferschpreches tzum Fahne .... Die Fersomme'ld Lodge

Ich ferschprech gedrei tzu sei tzu dem Fahne fun die fereenichte Schtaate fun Amerika, und des Land fer des er schteht, ae Land, Unnich Gott, ewich fareenicht, mit Freiheit Un Gerechtichkeet fer all.

Ruichie Minutt .... William W. Williams, Habtmon
Gabet .... Porra Russell Heintzelman
Ferbinnerei – die 78th Degree .... Donald Breininger
Musick darrich's Fescht Essa .... Die Rhinelanders

Es Fescht Essa

Lieder – Die Fersomme'ld Lodge .... Fohrsinger
Gross fon Northampton .... Thomas D. Reenock, Barya Maishder
Protocal Fohr Laisa .... Patrick J. Donmoyer, Schreiver
P'such Bekonnt Macha .... William Meck, UnnerHabtmon
Ebbes Shunsht .... William W. Williams, Habtmon
Lodge G'schefta .... Lee Haas, Grossdaadi Habtmon
Die Richdichie Grundsowdawg Wedder Berichta .... Bei da Grundsow Selvert
Nahayda und Tzucht – *un so emleidicha dinger* .... *#1 Rawdsleit*

Fescht Rade .... **Donald Peters**

Ehrwatt .... Die Fersomme'ld Lodge
Schluss un Letschte Wadde .... William W. Williams, Habtmon

Die Leschte Wadde
Leiwer Gott im Himmel drin,
Loss uns Deitsche was mir sin;
Und erhalt uns alle zeit
Unser Deitsche freelichkeit.

2014 Program from Groundhog Lodge #1.

An example of the pledge in Deitsch can be found in the 2014 program (*Ich ferschprech gedrei* . . .). In past years, the conflicts with Germany probably enhanced the emphasis on patriotism. At the ninth annual meeting of the Selinsgrove versammling, the *Snyder County Times* of January 16, 1941, stated, "In order that no one might misconstrue the purpose of the dinner or the motives of the men assembled, Dr. Woodruff proposed that the group go on record as affirming its loyalty to the U.S.A., disclaiming any connection with oppressor nations of Europe and condemning the persons guilty of war against humanity." According to the newspaper article, the resolution was "carried with a tremendous shout."[2] This meeting took place about a year before the Japanese attack on Pearl Harbor and Germany's declaration of war on the United States and reflects the participants' strong opposition to Hitler's activities in Europe. The introduction to Alvin Kemp's 1944 article about the versammlinge ends with this statement: "The thoughts embodied in the above poem and Flag salute, present the general purpose for which the Versammlinge were instituted and for which they will be perpetuated: Religious freedom, political freedom, social freedom, educational freedom and devotion to our country."[3] It is very possible that Kemp (or the volume's editors) wanted to make sure that readers understood the Pennsylvania Germans' commitment to the nation, especially during a war with Germany (see figures 8 and 9).

Solemn Minute
Ruichie Minutt in the 2014 program

At Groundhog Lodge #1 there is a brief interlude, during which the band usually plays solemn music, to remember the people who have died over the past year. This event has been listed in the annual programs since 1942. Many lodge members are elderly, and their numbers have been dwindling. Since the late 1990s, when I began attending meetings, several important leaders have passed away.

Prayer
Gebet in the 1934 program; *Gabet* in the 2014 program

Since the first lodge meeting in 1934, there has been a prayer, usually given by a pastor, again in the Deitsch language. Many other Pennsylvania

German heritage events and meetings also begin with a prayer. The prayer is usually spontaneous and short, thanking God for the food and the opportunity to join together to enjoy fellowship and celebrate Pennsylvania German culture.

Binding, Swearing the Oath
Ferbinnerrei in the 1934 program; *Ferbinnerei* in the 2014 program

Ferbinnerei (*Verbinnerei*) means "binding" or "uniting of new and old members," and the groundhog lodges use an oath of membership as a way to bind the members together and initiate new members. The oath, which is different every year, is a humorous statement in which the lodge members promise to follow certain behaviors in daily life that are characteristic of Pennsylvania German life and the groundhog. The men imitate the posture of a groundhog, standing with their forearms against their chests and hands out like paws. Some lodges may also have special ceremonies as part of the initiation of new members (see figures 3, 4, 23).

Lodge members often address each other as *Brieder* (brothers), reflecting the fact that many of the early founders and many of the current members are involved in fraternal lodges, especially the Freemasons, and much lodge activity derives from fraternal lodge activities, often with some humorous undertone. Every year Lodge #1 adds a "degree" for its members during the oath, like the "degrees" of Masonic membership. As of 2014, the lodge was at seventy-eight "degrees" (one for each year that the lodge has met, and excluding the three years the lodges did not meet during World War II).

Food, Dinner
Owet Essta in the 1934 program; *Es Fescht Essa* in the 2014 program

The food served at the meetings is usually general banquet fare, with some Pennsylvania German foods. At the first meeting of Lodge #1 in 1934, groundhog was served. Groundhog was part of many local diets through the middle of the twentieth century, and many older people still remember eating it. The second year, buffalo was served along with groundhog. Since then, however, the meals have been more standard. Today meals commonly include chicken, ham, sausage, potatoes, string beans, corn,

and filling (stuffing). There are some condiments that might be considered regional foods, including apple butter, applesauce, cottage cheese, tripe, and salad with bacon dressing. But at the meetings I have attended I have rarely found what I consider to be distinctive Pennsylvania German foods, such as pig's stomach, sauerkraut, apple dumplings, *Riwwelsupp*, or Pennsylvania German pot pie. The fare is to a large degree dependent upon the capabilities of the organizations where the meetings are held, the banquet halls of community buildings or fire companies. Although these organizations are in regions with large Pennsylvania German populations, they do not necessarily have the capability to cook many traditional Pennsylvania German foods.

A band plays during dinner (see figure 20). At present there are very few groups that still play Pennsylvania German songs, although in the past there were more. Many of these bands play Germanic/Bavarian brass music. For many years, until his retirement, Leroy Heffentrager's band was very popular. Leroy was the leader of a groundhog lodge, and he sang many songs in Deitsch.

Singing Songs

Lied—"Die Groundsow," "O Adoline," 'S Shpin Lied, "Die Boll Melinda" and *"Die Schnitzelbonk"* in the 1934 program; *Lieder—Die Fersomme'ld Lodge* in the 2014 program

In addition to "America," the participants sing other songs, all in Deitsch. The versammlinge are among the last occasions where Deitsch songs are still sung.[4] In 1934, songs were sung throughout different parts of the program; during my times at the meetings in the 1990s to the present, most songs were sung immediately following the dinner by everyone present (*Die Fersomme'ld Lodge*). There is a large repertoire of Deitsch songs, which can be divided into several broad categories based upon their sources, although there is some melding of these categories. The first category includes "traditional" songs that were brought over by the ancestors of the Pennsylvania Germans in the eighteenth century, or composed by Pennsylvania Germans after their settlement. Many of these songs were sung as part of Pennsylvania German daily life in the nineteenth century, but by the end of the twentieth century, they were mostly heard at festivals or special events, such as versammlinge. One of the most popular songs

at present is a humorous rendition of the trials of farm life, "Hei-Lie, Hei-Lo." Traditional Deitsch folk songs were well known to the founders of the lodges; indeed, William Troxell and Thomas Brendle, two of the most important people in the founding of the lodges and in the versammling movement more generally, made one of the first compilations of such songs. Nevertheless, a large number of songs sung at versammlinge are those translated from English, such as "O Adoline" ("Sweet Adeline") in 1934. I frequently have heard these songs sung in Deitsch at meetings: "Wait 'Till the Sun Shines, Nellie," and "She'll Be Coming Round the Mountain." Another popular song is "Die Ford Maschien" ("The Ford Automobile"), which describes the fine qualities of a Ford and the small amount of gas it requires. The Ford is favorably compared with an Overland, a Knox, and a Franklin, suggesting an early twentieth-century origin of the song, which might be derived from popular English-language songs of the period that praised Fords. Finally, there are songs brought by Germans who immigrated to the United States in the nineteenth and twentieth centuries and are derived from Standard German. Of these, one of the most popular at present is "Du, du liegst mir im Herzen."

A very popular song at all versammlinge is the "Schnitzelbank" song, which is usually sung to an accompanying chart or picture (see figure 19). It has been part of every versammlinge that I have attended and is often sung at other Pennsylvania German events. The song is listed in the program as the last event at the first lodge meeting in 1934; it appeared on the inside back cover of the program of Lodge #1 in 1964, and it has been on the inside or outside back cover of every program since then. The song, which was likely learned by Pennsylvania Germans from other German Americans and German immigrants in the nineteenth and twentieth centuries, seems a curious choice to be popular among Pennsylvania Germans in the 1930s, given that they often emphasized their differences from other German Americans and were very sensitive about their connections to Germany as a result of World War I. Nevertheless, it was and remains very popular.

Well known among German Americans throughout the United States, the song became incorporated into American popular culture. It appears in the 1932 Marx Brothers film *Horse Feathers*. It was sung by Joan Bennett, Cary Grant, and Gene Lockhart in the 1936 film *Wedding Present*. It was

sung in the 1953 Billy Wilder production of *Stalag 17*, in a scene in which American prisoners of war want to distract their German captors. It appeared in a 1956 episode of *I Love Lucy*. In 1957, Bill Haley and the Comets recorded a rock 'n' roll version. And in 1994, Steven Spielberg used the song in an episode of his popular cartoon show *Animaniacs*.[5] William Keel, a professor of German at the University of Kansas, has done extensive research on the song in Europe and the United States. He has found that it is performed in the United States in regions where Germans immigrated, especially in the Midwest. He has also found many examples of the song in German-speaking regions of Europe, and he dates written versions there to the early nineteenth century. In Basel, Switzerland, and Ellwagen, Germany, secret Schnitzelbank clubs traditionally sing songs at Shrovetide making fun of contemporary political issues; these events continue into the present day. In the United States, the song does not have any secret or political meanings. Keel suggests that in the United States there was an increase in the song's popularity after its performance at the 1933–34 International Exposition in Chicago and the standardization of an accompanying chart that includes pictures and words. Keel wryly comments that the Schnitzelbank charts used by Pennsylvania Germans, as opposed to other German Americans, often include nonstandard or variable spelling conventions, which I suspect is because the printers of these charts were translating Standard German into Deitsch spellings.[6]

Lodge Business

Ouslaiging, Der Regel Fohrlaisa, Der Regel Aw nemma in the 1934 program; *Gross fon Northampton, Protocal Fohr Laisa, P'such Bekonnt Macha, Ebbes Shunsht, Lodge G'schefta* in the 2014 program

There are several events that pertain to lodge business. At the first meeting in 1934, the lodge leader gave an explanation for the meeting (*Ouslaiging*). Then William Troxell, the main organizer, read the new rules of the organization (*Der Regel Fohrlaisa*), and the lodge leader asked the members to accept them (*Regel Aw nemma*). In recent years, Lodge #1 has asked the mayor of Northampton, where the lodge held meetings for many years, to give a brief talk (*Gross fon Northampton*). The secretary then reads a report about the activities of the lodge during the previous year (*Protocal Fohr Laisa*).

This report includes a discussion of minutes from the organizational meetings of the lodge's board, a statement about finances, and a brief recounting of last year's meeting. Many of the lodge's activities include recording lodge activities. This seems to emphasize the importance of the events, but also struck me as somewhat playful in its seriousness. There is other lodge business in addition to reading the minutes. At the meetings, there is a brief introduction of visiting dignitaries, such as leaders from other lodges or notable people who are closely involved in Pennsylvania German activities (*P'such Bekonnt Macha*). The lodge leader may have some brief presentations or ask certain visitors to make short talks (*Ebbes Shunsht*). The members and the officers of the board are nominated and elected by those in attendance (*Lodge G'schefta* in program for 2014).

The Groundhog's Weather Prediction
Die Wedder oussicht in the 1934 program; *Die Richdichie Grundsowdawg Wedder Berichta* in the 2014 program

There is a report from a person who claims to be observing the groundhog to find out whether the groundhog sees his shadow. In recent years, this has been played on a tape recorder or over a loudspeaker. The report is an amusing description of groundhog actions, often with humorous allusions to people involved in the lodges.

Performances, Skits, and Drama
Shtick—Die Ombtsleit Om Grunsow Loch in the 1934 program; *Nahayda und Tzucht* in the 2014 program

In addition to several short skits or performances (*Schtick*), the first meeting of Lodge #1 in 1934 featured an extended play about the groundhog, written by the Reverend Thomas Brendle, *Die Ombtsleit Om Grunsow Loch* (The lodge officers at the groundhog hole), in which the officers of the lodge gather outside a groundhog hole to wait for his prediction. Every year since then, Lodge #1 has featured a humorous performance, and most versammlinge of all types include theatrical performances. In recent years, yearly skits have been performed at Lodge #1 under the generic title of *Nahayda und Tzucht* (Nonsense and noise). These skits will be discussed in more detail in chapter 4 (see figures 32–34).

The Main Speaker and Speeches

Rade in the 1934 program; *Fescht Rade* in the 2014 program

There is always an extended speech or several speeches (*Rade, Fescht Rade*). The first lodge meeting in 1934 had three speakers: William Troxell (listed as Pumpernickle Bill), Edwin Fogel, and Thomas Brendle. Troxell was the real motivator and organizer of the lodge meetings. Brendle was a German Reformed pastor and a close friend of Troxell's who made very important contributions to collecting and recording Pennsylvania German folk culture. Edwin Fogel was a professor of German at the University of Pennsylvania who wrote several books about Pennsylvania German folklore.[7] In past years, there tended to be two or more speakers: one was often humorous, and the other was more serious in content. More recently most gatherings have only one main speaker, the *Fescht Rade*. The most popular speakers use humor to deliver a serious message. These speeches will be discussed in more detail in chapter 5 (see figures 7, 30).

Word of Honor

Ehrwatt in the 2014 program

Starting in 1993, a Pennsylvania German "Word of Honor" has been read toward the end of the meetings at Lodge #1. It was written by John Bensing, a retired educator.

Pennsylfaanisch Deitsch Ehrwatt	[*Pennsylvania German Word of Honor*
Ich bin schtolz fun unser Pennsylfaanisch Deitsche Faahne un aa die Mudder Schprooch, fum Schiff, os unserer Foreldre doh gebrocht hot, fun die Karich, os Uns, uff'm rechde Paad halt, fum Blug, os uns uff'm Land gholfe hot, fun die Kunscht, os uns Zeit gebt fer Dinger du os mir gleiche, fum Wagga, os uns iwwer des gross Land genumme	I am proud of our Pennsylvania German Flag; and also the Mother Tongue; of the Ship, that brought our Forefathers here; the Church, that keeps us on the right path; of the Plow, that helped us on the Land; of the Arts, that give us time to do the things we enjoy; of the Wagon, that took us across this large land; the Colors, red, white, and blue, that

hot, fun die Farewe, rot, weiss, un blo, os weisse os mir aller erscht Amerikaanisch sin, un fum Schlisselschtee, os uns Pennsylfaanisch Deitsche beinanner halt fer die Ewichkeit.

show we are first of all Americans, and of the Keystone, that keeps us Pennsylvania Germans together for Posterity.]8

The "Word of Honor" reiterates the meeting's main themes and is partly based upon the images on the Pennsylvania German flag discussed in chapter 2 (see figure 13).

Conclusion and Last Words
Schluss un Letschte Wadde in the 2014 program

The first program from 1934 lists the "Schnitzelbank" song as the last item of the meeting. More recently, the final words have been the following long-standing motto of the lodges and other versammlinge, which is recited at the conclusion of every meeting, and is found at the end of the program from 2014:

Leiwer9 Gott im Himmel drin,
Loss uns Deitsche was mir sin;
Und erhalt uns alle zeit
Unser Deitsche freelichkeit

[*Dear God in Heaven,
Let us Deitsche be what we are;
And preserve for all time
Our Deitsche merriment*]

This verse is found on the inside back cover of the program from the lodge's first meeting in 1934. It appeared on the outside back cover of programs from 1936 until the early 2000s, when it was moved to the program page and replaced on the back cover with the "Schnitzelbank" song. As discussed in the previous chapter, the first two lines of the saying are on the Pennsylvania German flag (see figures 6, 13).

In most of the versammlinge there is no alcohol. I heard some criticism of versammlinge that did serve alcohol because the audience became distracted from the evening's events. The people attending these meetings are definitely not opposed to drinking alcohol, but they do not see it as necessary for their "Deitsche merriment."

Past and Present: Ritualized Events with Contemporary Content

The structure of the versammlinge has essential elements, including heritage, the Deitsch language, patriotism, religion, food, song, drama, a message, and a farewell that asks God to allow the people to remain as they are and keep their merriment. The similarity of events across time has become ritualistic, as events are repeated year after year. The groundhog lodges compound this ritualistic, element with the ceremony surrounding the groundhog, including the dramatic entry of the groundhog, posing as a groundhog during the oath of membership, a weather report from the groundhog, as well as many references throughout the evening. Versammling events are recorded in minutes, photographs, tape recordings (and more recently videos), and reported in regional newspapers, these representations themselves contributing to the ceremonial and ritual nature of the events. The versammlinge were new events in 1933, but for more than eighty years they have preserved a standardized format. The similarities across the years and meetings create a core of shared experiences that cut across time. The gatherings use theatrical and speaking styles that are grounded in the nineteenth and early twentieth centuries, and in this sense are themselves traditional. Within the traditional speaking styles and the similar format, however, there is constant innovation in the content as current events and concerns are woven into the skits and speeches. And many of the dramatic events, especially the ceremonialism about groundhogs, strike me as containing an undercurrent of very modern irony, suggesting that the participants use these meetings to create an implicit tension between past and present to better understand and manage both. This tension is expressed in the events' theatricality.

DIE TZAED YAIRLICH FERSOMMLUNG UNS FESHT FON DA GRUNDSOW LODGE NUMMER AINS ON DER LECHAW

GRUNDSOW-WEDDER BROFATE

BUD TAMBLYN

4.

Theatricality

PERFORMING TRADITION

From my very first versammling, I have been fascinated by the theatricality and drama that is involved in the events, especially in the meetings of the groundhog lodges. Grown and mostly elderly men treat the groundhog with deference and ceremony, at one point, during the *Ferbinnerei*, raising both hands as paws and swearing loyalty to the lodge membership and groundhog. This is done by people who live in a modern, industrialized society structured by constant innovation and complex technology, a society that I normally associate with emotional restraint and rationality. Almost every versammling has a humorous skit. In the first skit I saw, Carl Snyder, the normally reserved, serious, laconic leader of Lodge #1, played the role of a lecherous quack doctor who cured patients by transferring their ailments through a machine to one of his assistants. His lechery toward his nurse was made more hilarious because the nurse was played by an elderly man dressed as a woman and wearing a long blonde wig. The more people the doctor saw, the more infirm his assistant became.[1] The skit played upon several themes that struck me as an ironic view of the modern and the past which I found at many other gatherings: a modern

machine that can transfer diseases in an old-fashioned way; the foolish man who is willing to receive these ailments; the presentation of a doctor, normally a respected professional, as both a quack and lecherous; and finally the implicit wink at the audience that no one there is so stupid and gullible as to believe such nonsense.

We live in a time when television, films, and cable programming present highly commercialized and polished dramatic events. In these media, dramatic acting is done by professionals as part of electronic productions that use sophisticated technology to camouflage staging and create a veneer of realism. But the events at the versammlinge reflect their roots in the late nineteenth and early twentieth centuries, when there were many popular dramatic events that were more spontaneous and personal, at local community events, fraternal organizations, community bands, neighborhood taverns, and street corners. At the versammlinge the staging is explicit, and the events emphasize a rough spontaneity, as opposed to the rehearsed, manufactured, and smooth "spontaneity" of modern media. Rehearsals are minimal, scripting is limited, and improvisation is frequent.

Humor and theatricality are especially prominent at the groundhog lodge meetings, where the entire event is structured around a notion of the groundhog predicting the weather, coupled with a playful incorporation of fraternal lodge ceremonies. The highly repetitive, ritual structure of the event enhances this theatricality. At Lodge #1, an eight-foot-tall papier-mâché groundhog stands at the front of the meeting room. In previous years, a man climbed inside and walked the groundhog in on rollers, stopping to talk with members of the audience. There are colorful wall hangings, including a banner, a wheel with spokes on which the names of the board members of the lodge are written, a *Taufschein* (a traditional Pennsylvania German baptismal certificate) commemorating the lodge's founding date, and a sign with a groundhog forbidding the use of English (see figures 5, 12, 14, 16, 17, 18, 22).

At the very beginning of the meetings of Lodge #1, the lights are dimmed, the band plays rousing music, and a groundhog inside a case is carried on poles into the hall by the lodge's officers, who are wearing top hats, and placed at the front of the room. During the *Ferbinnerei* (oath taking), everyone stands, holds their arms to their chests and puts out their

hands, like a standing groundhog, and promises to obey the rules of lodge membership and the groundhog (see figures 3, 4, 23). In some meetings, new members are initiated with special ceremonies. In 1937, new members of Lodge #1 were given a bottle of milk with a nipple and told to suck from it. A newspaper described the scene: "Doctors, lawyers, ministers, mechanics and farmers alike shared the milk that was served to aid them in growing up with the rest of the groundhogs present."[2]

Spontaneity is an important element. Skits are collaboratively developed as they are rehearsed, and ad libbing occurs during the performance. In 2013, Bill Meck, the assistant leader of Lodge #1, in a spur-of-the-moment decision on the day of the versammling, rented a groundhog costume and went around the crowd greeting people in it (see figure 33).

The theatricality can extend beyond the meeting halls. Lodge #16 has a special public event on February 2 in which a stuffed groundhog is pulled across the Jordan Creek in Allentown and then the lodge leader presents the groundhog's weather prediction. In 2013 and 2014, crowds of about two hundred people, including men, women, and children, gathered early in the morning to witness the event, which started at 7 A.M. Coffee and cookies were set out. The lodge officers were present in top hats, and an American flag and the Pennsylvania German flag stood on a little podium. The crowd was led in the Pledge of Allegiance, singing "America" and "She'll Be Coming Round the Mountain" and other songs, all in Deitsch with English translations for the mostly non-Deitsch-speaking audience. The groundhog was pulled across the creek, and one of the men interpreted his weather prediction, first in Deitsch and then in English (see figure 35).

The Skit

Most versammlinge include some kind of skit, which along with the main speech (*Fescht Rade*) is considered one of the most important events of the evening. There is a long tradition of skits and plays in the Deitsch language. Harry Hess Reichard traces the origin of Deitsch plays to puppet theater and comic acts of the early nineteenth century. William Fetterman suggests that another influence was the games played as part of nineteenth-century community farming events, such as *Mosch Riehre* (stirring

the mush). In the late nineteenth century, Pennsylvania German writers began to write plays in Deitsch and to translate plays from English into Deitsch, including scenes from Shakespeare and Gilbert and Sullivan's *H.M.S. Pinafore*. Deitsch playwriting took off in the 1920s and 1930s. In 1928, Clarence Iobst wrote a humorous Deitsch play, *En Quart Millich un en Halb Beint Raahm* (A quart of milk and a half pint of cream), for a performance at Emmaus High School outside of Allentown. The play became extremely popular and was soon performed throughout the region. Deitsch playwriting contests were sponsored by the city of Allentown in the 1930s. From 1944 until 1954, Clarence Rahn wrote a weekly Deitsch radio program, *Asseba un Sabina*, that presented a humorous rendition of a fictional farm couple and was very popular among Deitsch speakers in the region.[3]

In many Pennsylvania German Deitsch plays, including Iobst's play and *Asseba un Sabina*, the roles of women are performed by men. With a few exceptions, this is true of the groundhog lodge meetings. Since many of the situations include friction between men and women, the lechery of men, and seductive women, the humor is enhanced by men acting the roles of women (see figure 32).

Much of the content of Pennsylvania German drama, including that performed at versammlinge, follows patterns set in the general popular culture of nineteenth-century America, including vaudeville. William Fetterman, in his study of the origins of Pennsylvania German plays, writes, "Most plays have not presented a scene from contemporary life, nor have most plays been concerned with what we would call 'folklore.' The typical dialect play is often a nostalgic comedy employing the playwriting formula of the nineteenth-century farce or burlesque play."[4]

Nineteenth-century formulas may seem dated today, but are important sources for much of the expressive humor in versammlinge. Many of the founders of the versammling movement were raised in the late nineteenth century, and their memories of Pennsylvania German life are based upon their childhood experiences before the introduction of radio and later forms of electronic media and the widespread use of technology such as the automobile, electricity, telephone, and plumbing.

Albert Buffington, another scholar of Deitsch plays and language, has described the importance of humor in Pennsylvania German drama, and he

finds that it is preferable if there is a message: "If a play makes a Pennsylvania 'Dutchman' laugh until the tears come down, then he will generally regard it as a good play. However, most Pennsylvania 'Dutchmen' will like the play even better if, in addition and beneath the froth, there runs a vein of sound, though unobtrusive, philosophy."[5] Buffington also offers insights into the presentation of the past in many of the Pennsylvania German theatrical performances, including at the versammlinge, noting the underlying irony of viewing the past from the perspective of the present: "Even though many Pennsylvania German plays take place in the past, e.g., 'fuffzich Yaahr zerick' [fifty years ago], there has been no nostalgic yearning for 'the good old days,' such as one frequently finds expressed in the Pennsylvania German poetry laid in the same period. On the contrary, the audience has been led to look upon the past with an air of superiority, laughing at the peculiar ways, the odd garments, the queer ideas, the outmoded thinking of the fathers."[6]

At many groundhog lodge plays, the past is unsophisticated and naïve, but the present is overly complicated, confusing, and, if looked through the discerning lens of the past, perhaps even more ridiculous. The audience laughs at the Dutchy country rubes, but they also laugh at the convolutions of modern life. A tension is created between past and present, from which the audience is able to see both in sharp contrast and view both with a somewhat jaundiced eye.

Many of the plays center around the activities of the groundhog, and the imagery surrounding it seems to me symbolic of that same tension. I doubt that anyone still believes that the groundhog predicts the weather, but the Pennsylvania Germans are willing to pretend for an evening that they hold these rural beliefs of a previous time. They honor a humble predictor of the weather in their folk tradition and at the same time realize their distance from such traditional beliefs.

At the first meeting of Lodge #1 in 1934, the Reverend Thomas Brendle composed a skit concerning a group of men who go searching for the groundhog to learn his weather prediction. The groundhog, who is nursing a sore tail that was shot the previous summer by one of the men while hunting, is reluctant to leave his hole, despite his wife's nagging. In the following scene, the men come upon the groundhog. The men are from the board (*Raad*), and their real names are used:[7]

REV. BRENDLE
Mei guder freind, hier stehn m'r un welle mit d'r schwetze.
Long war d'r winder, un kalt d'r naddlich wind,
Tief war d'r schnee, un hard d'r bodde gfrore.
Mied un satt sin m'r mit dem unschietlich wedder,
Sag, grundsau, sag wann wadd d'r friehling kumme?

[*My good friend. Here we stand and want to talk with you.*
The winter was long and the north wind cold,
The snow was deep, and the ground frozen hard.
We are tired with this unpredictable weather,
Speak, groundhog, say when the spring will come.]

OLD GROUNDHOG—J. E. LENTZ
Wanns re'ert, wadds nass
Wanns schneet, wadds weiss,
Wanns friert, gebts eis,
Is d'r winder ferbei, muss's frieh yohr do sei.

[*When it rains, it gets wet*
When it snows, it turns white,
When it freezes, it is icy,
When winter is over, spring must be here.]

ALL
Jar, Jar, sell is recht.

[*Yes, yes, that is right.*]

REV. BRENDLE
E'r wees es allrecht.

[*He knows it, all right.*]

PUMPERNICKEL BILL
Sell hen m'r jo schun all gewisst. Frog weider.

[*We already knew all that. Ask some more.*]

    This equivocation about the future weather is quite common in many of the predictions that take place throughout the evening's activities. The groundhog is the king of weather prophecy, although his predictions are often undercut by Delphic ambiguity. Eventually, in the play, the groundhog realizes it is a sunny day and so he must return to his hole to wait for winter, something he does not relish because it means more weeks with a nagging wife. Similar battles between the sexes are a common source of humor in many of the evening's activities.

SERIOUS NONSENSE

OLD GROUNDHOG—J. E. LENTZ

Sag m'r. Was dheedet i'r dhu wann d'ir sechs woche imme loch lewe misst mit re alde besse, gretzige, bissiche grundsau, ass dich in dei schwans beisst ass halwer abg-schoose war letsch summer von so 'm langlechticher bauersbu.

[*Tell me. What can you do when you must live six more weeks in the hole with an old angry, complaining, biting groundhog who bites you in the tail that was half shot off last summer by a Lancaster farm boy.*]

Over the years a recurring theme in the skits has been a comparison of the groundhog's weather-predicting ability with that of its many rivals. An obvious rival is Punxsutawney Phil, who was sent to the gallows in a 1972 skit (see figure 3).[8] In Lehigh County, there was a "goosebone man," Willoughby Troxell, a relative of William "Pumpernickel Bill" Troxell, who claimed to be able to predict the weather with the bones of a goose (see figure 30).[9] The *Allentown Morning Call* ran several articles about him and sometimes compared his predictions with those coming from the groundhog lodges. Many of the early plays ridicule the goose's ability to predict the weather. Several plays are set in a classroom, with the goose given the role of dunce.[10] William Fetterman traces many of these school skits to humorous presentations of classrooms in vaudeville acts in the early twentieth century, performed by such leading comics as the Marx Brothers, Mae West, Eddie Cantor, and Bert Lahr.[11]

Sometimes the skits are mostly slapstick, generally with a sexual or scatological point. But even these often include some commentary about the past and present. In one performance that I attended, a husband eats too much of his wife's sauerkraut and hot dogs and has to make a visit to the outhouse. Smoke starts coming from the outhouse as the man passes gas. A neighbor comes by and lights a pipe, which ignites the gas and leads to an explosion. As the husband, tattered and burned, comes out of the outhouse, he compliments his wife on her excellent sauerkraut. Bill Meck, the writer of this skit and of many other recent performances, told me that he wanted to remind people of the past times when outhouses were much more common. The idea came to him after he was talking with a construction contractor who complained that in his younger days, he never felt

reluctant to use the family outhouse on construction jobs, but now that everyone had indoor plumbing he was reluctant to ask the homeowners to use their more fashionable facilities. In another recent skit, a group of hunters are in a hunting cabin. The arrival of a man from New York in a camouflage outfit contrasts with the Pennsylvania Germans in simple attire, playing upon a recurring theme of the simple salt-of-the-earth Pennsylvania German in contrast to the wealthier but affected outsider. In 2013, a skit was performed using a script that had been performed for the versammling thirty years earlier. The skit was based upon a series of humorous events during a day in the life of a Pennsylvania German family. The roles of women were played by the wives of lodge members. A doctor arrives to treat the husband, who has a pain in his rear. The goggle-glassed doctor, whose clothing and behavior make him look like a quack, injects the farmer's rear with a huge needle, sending the farmer jumping (see figure 34). At the performance I saw, there was some contemporary ad libbing that brought the old script up to date, all the while still playing on a humorous contrast between the past and present. At the end of his visit the doctor ad libbed about the farmer's health care plan, a clear reference to contemporary issues that was made funnier by the setting, which was clearly from many years ago.[12] A pastor appeared and was offered a chicken (there are common Pennsylvania German jokes about gluttonous pastors who come for a chicken dinner). The pastor, played by a real pastor, ad libbed a complaint that all he is ever offered is chicken. Why doesn't he ever get served pork or steak?

    The presence of an audience enhances the event. When I attended the dress rehearsal of the skit, it seemed a little flat, and I feared that it would not be well received. During the presentation before a live audience, however, I felt the skit went very well. Perhaps the actors were livelier and more creative in their ad libbing, but I also think that the performance was enhanced by an audience that appreciated the event and responded enthusiastically.

    Current events are often incorporated into the skits. In 1934, the versammling in Selinsgrove included a short satirical impersonation of Adolf Hitler.[13] In 1946 at Groundhog Lodge #1, there was a humorous skit about capturing, trying, and executing Hitler, who was found hiding as a skunk

in a large hole.¹⁴ In 1973, there was a humorous mock protest by women demanding to be allowed to enter the groundhog lodges (see figure 31). The protest, which was planned by the lodge's leaders and staged by their wives, played upon the contemporaneous effort of the women's movement to expand the rights of women.¹⁵ It was temporarily resolved but recurred in 1974. In a skit performed in 1975, during the energy crisis and gasoline shortage, a rabbit and her three children take over a groundhog hole. The groundhog wants the hole back. A wealthy Arab sheik arrives who wants to buy all the groundhog holes for a thousand dollars each to store his excess oil. Henry Kissinger, at that time the U.S. secretary of state, who had been involved in extensive negotiations with the Soviet Union, China, and Vietnam, enters and works out a solution (in Deitsch) keeping the holes for groundhogs.¹⁶ In 1980, the groundhog again faced the energy crisis by proposing the use of applejack in gas tanks or greater use of bikes. (Continuing the theme, the main speaker, the Reverend Richard Wolf, warned that the crisis of peoples' lack of individual energy in their everyday lives was a bigger problem than the energy crisis in gasoline shortages.)¹⁷

During presidential election years, the groundhog is often proposed for president. After the election of Barack Obama, a telephone call was played during the meeting in which the new president discussed in Deitsch his Pennsylvania German ancestors, continuing the theme from seventy-five years earlier when a telegram written in Deitsch by President Roosevelt was read to the first versammling in Selinsgrove.

In 1979, in a relatively rare look at historical rather than current events, the groundhog mediated a dispute about the Walking Purchase, in which the Penn family took land from Native Americans.¹⁸ In 1949, the skit satirized powwowing, a traditional curing practice that was widely used in the region.¹⁹ Today many older people still have stories of cures given to them by a powwow doctor. It is also somewhat controversial for its alternative approach to healing, and perhaps more troubling, some associate it with the use of witchcraft (*Hexerei*) in the past.

As noted above, the groundhog lodge skits often present a tension between an unsophisticated past and an overly complicated present. In 1966, an electronic device was brought in to predict the weather, but before it could operate it went up in smoke. The commentator remarked, "Science

was again discredited by solid folklore." In 1967, a lodge member brought in a machine to forecast the weather, but it too malfunctioned, spewing out programming cards all over the stage. The modern age of mechanization overwhelmed the weathercaster, and someone consulted the groundhog to get an old-fashioned and more reliable weather prediction.[20] More recently, a country rube and his wife wanted to see Punxsutawney Phil on Groundhog Day. He planned to fly, but was confounded by the post-9/11 security measures at the airport, which required him to take off his smelly socks and shoes. Eventually, he and his wife gave up and simply took off in a hot air balloon. Another skit was woven around the Marcellus shale deposits, which are currently being drilled in Pennsylvania and are often seen as a new boon to the economy. There are no deposits in the Pennsylvania German region, but Bill Meck, the skit writer, was hunting in a region that was being drilled when he came up with his idea for a script. Two men meet at a restaurant, and one proposes that the fumes coming from groundhog holes might be signs of gas in their region. They decide to ask someone to come and drill in the area. A Texan arrives with a suitcase overflowing with money and a contract that is several feet of old computer paper. After some doubts, he signs the contract with the Dutchmen and passes them the money. When he asks to see the gas, a curtain rises and the gas is seen as being from groundhog holes. Knowing that there is no real natural gas, the two Dutchmen then run away with the money. Another recent skit plays off a recent proposal to allow Pennsylvanians to hunt on Sundays. A group of groundhogs are sitting around lamenting the new law and the fact that they will no longer have at least one day off from worrying about being shot. Eventually they decide to conduct a telephone campaign, contacting people to convince legislators not to pass a new law that would allow hunting on Sundays. They start with old-fashioned telephones, but eventually switch to cell phones and finally text messages to try to convince people to keep the prohibition of hunting on Sunday. The skit sets the humor of talking groundhogs against the modern technology of cell phones and text messages.

Bill Meck got another idea for a skit during a meeting of a lodge board. At the end of the meeting, the officers, most in their seventies and eighties, were hurrying to leave for some business errand or job. Meck started

laughing and thought it could be humorous to have a skit about a group of elderly men who should all be retired and collecting Social Security and instead all have to hurry back to work. The theme pointed to both the trials of contemporary life and the value that Pennsylvania Germans place on hard work.

The skits are almost always written in collaboration with the performers. A writer proposes a rough script or some general ideas, which are then worked out and elaborated in rehearsals. One scriptwriter was notorious for waiting until the last moment to write his scripts, causing anxious moments for the lodge leader and performers. The performances themselves derive energy from the spontaneity and collective contributions of the cast. For many years, Don Breininger developed the ideas for the Lehigh Valley Fersommling, a general versammling for both men and women.[21] Like other skit writers, Don incorporates contemporary themes into his skits, including current events or formats from popular television shows. Don emphasizes that he never actually writes a script; rather, people work spontaneously and collaboratively in developing an idea: "We don't write them out. People ask us for copies of the script. We don't have copies of the script. We get together with an idea and then I put it together and I give a responsibility to one person and something else to another."

The spontaneous, improvised, and collective aspect of skit production is important. For a few years in the early 2000s, there were Pennsylvania German skits performed on a local radio station. One man fondly remembered the composition of these scripts, mostly through interaction and ad libbing. He discussed one popular radio skit, "Why Do Kamikaze Pilots Wear Helmets?," and the humor that arose as the cast developed a series of jokes around this theme. Another time, I heard lodge board members recall humorous events in the skits of past years, including the mistakes and surprises, such as when a performer drank from a glass that was supposed to be full of water but that a prankster had filled with gin instead.

Some of the performances are more serious and involve more staging. For many years, Irwin Klinger composed popular skits for the annual versammling in Lykens, Dauphin County. He describes his skits as

"purely for local consumption, for entertainment at versammlings and picnics, with as much local humor as possible woven into them." In his play *Wie es als war*, he uses a stage technique in which two elderly men on one side of the stage recall humorous events from their youth, which are enacted on the other side of the stage. Klinger's plays were popular for their representation of the past and were among the more serious efforts in this genre.[22]

The performative and dramatic qualities are expressed in a variety of forms besides drama. Lodge #1 suspended meetings from 1943–45, during the war. In 1943, the lodge sent out a colorful broadside announcing that there would be no meeting for the year and wishing for the demise of Hitler so they could hold their meeting in 1944. The broadside was done in the form of a "New Year's Wish," a traditional Pennsylvania German event in which people move from house to house making wishes for the New Year (see figure 9). The broadside concluded,

Ow'r hoffa die Grundsow kon uns fohrshtella,	[*It is our hope that the groundhog can foresee*
Dos bis '44 rum kumt, is der Hitler unnich da wella.	*That by the time 1944 arrives, Hitler will have slipped beneath the sea.*]

As in the theatrical skits, current events are often humorously incorporated into the program covers: health insurance, pollution, space travel, energy sources, current politics, and modern technology are topics. Some of the covers contrast the past and present, others refer to contemporary events, and some do both. Lodge #1 often has creative and colorful program covers. Every cover includes two scenes: one of winter and another of summer, to represent the groundhog's prediction. Another frequent theme is the contrast of the complexities of contemporary life with a simpler past. Winter and summer, past and present play off one another. In the program cover for 1958, winter and summer are represented by pictures on the earth, while a rocket crashes into the moon. The scene might be a response to the Soviet Union's Sputnik, the first artificial satellite, which was launched in October 1957 (see figure 24). On the 1962 cover, a woman groundhog is cooking a traditional Pennsylvania German meal,

Rivla soup (*Riwwelsupp*), on a coal stove. Out the window, summer and winter are depicted in images of missiles and mushroom clouds, probably a reference to the arms race between the United States and Soviet Union. There is a troubling contrast between the old-fashioned, homey, humble groundhog and the modern fearful world of destructive technology (figure 25). The cover in 1965 keeps the contrast of old and new as the groundhog is in a burrow watching a television with a split screen depicting scenes from summer and winter (figure 26). In 1970, the groundhog is on the moon, likely a reference to the first American moon landing in the summer of 1969 (see figure 27). In 1979, there was rapid inflation, and the scene of summer shows the groundhog bringing a wheelbarrow piled with money to a country store, while the scene of winter shows him leaving the store with a small basket in the wheelbarrow (figure 28). In 1999, President Bill Clinton was embroiled in a sex scandal with a White House intern, Monica Lewinsky. The program cover shows the president and the groundhog outside the White House (one side is winter, the other summer), and the groundhog asks, "Where is this young woman Monica?" An image of Monica wearing her famous beret is in a bubble above the president's head (figure 29).

The Origins in Nineteenth-Century Theatrical Traditions

The versammling skits at least partly derive from nineteenth-century theatrical, vaudeville, and minstrel traditions. In the 1930s, about the time that the versammling movement was developed, Constance Rourke, one of the first scholars to seriously study the popular culture of common, ordinary Americans, identified popular, humorous, theatrical traditions in American life that reflect important cultural themes. Rourke showed how these traditions developed throughout the nineteenth century among the common people and argued that they are much more important for understanding American character than the formal performances of high theater in urban centers, which were derived from Europe and supported by the highbrow, wealthy elites. For Rourke, this indigenous American tradition represented the perspective of the rural, common, humble people, and its humor often opposed them to the pretentious, sophisticated, urban, and

wealthy. Rourke traced this humorous theatrical tradition through literary and political figures including Whitman, Melville, Lincoln, and Twain, and argued that it continued in the twentieth century in urban ethnic humor. More recently and in a similar vein, Robert Toll, another scholar of popular theater, wrote that the origins of important trends in American theatricality can be found in the Jacksonian era, which emphasized the virtues and interests of the common person. Theater developed that had no detailed scripts and drew upon folk stories. This became an important part of American theatrical traditions until the twentieth century, when radio and television became so pervasive.[23]

In this and many other respects, the versammlinge preserve nineteenth- and early twentieth-century performance traditions that were developed before the electronic mass media of radio, television, and cable programming. The theatricality is especially pronounced at the groundhog lodge meetings, which combine the ritualistic drama of a pseudo-fraternal lodge organization with the celebration of the groundhog. The lodges literally dramatize the tension between a past that is unsophisticated but somehow feels more authentic as opposed to a present that for all its advanced technology seems convoluted and superficial. For a few hours, the drama allows participants to leave the cool detachment of modern life and replace it with more emotional, personal, dramatic, and animated forms of expression.

The presentation of the past simplifies and stereotypes the Pennsylvania German of past times. Their ancestors were neither so uneducated nor so inept as some skits suggest. This simplified past, as Alfred Buffington suggests, can be laughed at by the audience, which has seen and appreciated many changes over the course of their lives. These Pennsylvania Germans are not calling for a return to the past, but they are troubled by many of the complexities and absurdities of the present. The performances themselves are opportunities to participate in spontaneous theater. In the present era of highly technical, commercialized media presentations, the versammlinge produce their own performances, often incorporating a modern world into their Deitsch language and personal expressive idiom. The skits create a theatrical "time out" from the complex modern world that also allows for a personal and humorous interpretation of that

world. A tribute to the more traditional life of the nineteenth century is expressed in a medium of the time. These themes of the contrasts between past and present, the authentic common person and superficial sophisticate, are also displayed in the meeting's main speech, the subject of the next chapter.

Grundsow Lodge Nummer Ains
ON DA LECHAW

5.

The Message of the Versammlinge

THE REVEREND CLARENCE RAHN AND THE MAIN SPEECH

Every versammling includes a speech, given by the main or banquet speaker (*Fescht Rade*), that lasts about twenty to thirty minutes. In earlier times, there were often several talks, at least one more serious and another more humorous. In recent years, there is usually one main speech, which should combine both humorous and serious elements. Some speakers who are recognized for their abilities often make the rounds giving numerous speeches to different versammlinge throughout the Deitsch-speaking region. Much of the speech's style and humor has origins in nineteenth-century American comic traditions, and the most popular speakers exemplify the insight of the common person as opposed to the sophistry of the elite.

Everyone described the Reverend Clarence Rahn as the exemplary speaker. Rahn, a popular minister in the German Reformed Church, was widely admired for his use of a wealth of life experiences, as a laborer, teacher, inventor, farmer, and pastor, to humorously communicate a message or "text" in which he delivered insight into human behavior, often with praise for traditional Pennsylvania German practices and character (see figures 7, 30). He avoided complex philosophical or theological concepts, preferring simple,

direct messages that appealed to the common person. The most popular speakers from 1995–2015, when I was learning about the versammlinge, were directly influenced by Rahn; they emulated his style, took his advice when they were starting as speakers, and were inspired by his encouragement.[1]

Although speeches are often humorous and may be peppered with some sexual innuendo, it is important that they have a theme, message, or "text." Don Yoder has compared these versammling speeches to the *Waerdagsbreddich* (weekday sermons) Pennsylvania German preachers used to make.[2] Many of the most popular speakers are pastors, and other popular versammling speakers have adopted this style. Occasionally speakers use a lot of off-color humor with explicit sexual imagery, but most people, including the most popular speakers, are clear that they disapprove of this kind of humor. It is frequently said that the best speakers are "earthy, not dirty."

Explaining versammling meetings in the early 1950s, Russell Gilbert, a professor at Susquehanna University, a fluent speaker of Deitsch and one of the organizers of the first versammling in Selinsgrove, described the speech in terms that are still essential sixty years later:

> A philosophy of life needs to permeate the humor before a favorable and lasting impression can be made. A deep thought has to lie subtly encased in the witty and humorous before the audience can feel the satisfaction requirement of good speaking.[3]

> Ideas glorifying Pennsylvania German accomplishments in his own *Mundart*, simple, unhewn and unsophisticated, can engender uncommon enthusiasm for even the commonplace.[4]

> The common ground, readily established, eases the fulfillment of purpose. Well-accepted ideas of Pennsylvania German morality, such as thrift, simplicity, industriousness, reliance upon God, personal responsibility rather than a dependence upon government and outside agencies, family virtues, interest in the church, and hatred of hypocrisy and exhibition—these and many others rejuvenate the Pennsylvania German zest for living even in trying times. The effect of these speeches is equal to the aesthetic cathartic influence of a great play.[5]

Clarence Rahn and the Message of the Meeting

Rahn was often described as the Will Rogers or Mark Twain of the Pennsylvania Germans.[6] He appreciated the reference to Will Rogers but, as a Christian pastor, not that to Mark Twain because of Twain's caustic comments about religion and Christianity. These references, however, reflect a very important theme in Rahn's talks. The content of the message often praises traditional Pennsylvania German values, and the form of the delivery recalls a time before radio, television, and most recently digital media, when face-to-face conversation and oral interaction were the prevalent forms of communication. During those times, it was possible and even common to make a good living through speaking engagements. Twain was a noted speaker, as was Rogers, who in addition to personal appearances was able to translate his folksy delivery into a very popular show in the early days of radio. Twain, in his early and better-known writings (*Roughing It*, *The Innocents Abroad*, *Life on the Mississippi*, and *Huckleberry Finn*), and Rogers represent a humorous philosophy of the common person that goes to the core of many important Pennsylvania German values and themes expressed in the gatherings.[7]

Rahn espoused a simple, down-to-earth philosophy that emphasized the importance of ordinary people. One of his most popular talks, given in both English and Deitsch, used a wheelbarrow as a metaphor for the common person's life. Rahn explained: "I point out that a wheelbarrow is sort of symbol of life—nothing happens unless someone takes the personal responsibility to push. Talking and promoting doesn't move a wheelbarrow. But a wheelbarrow is very useful to haul out old, worn-out ideas and bring in new supplies of enthusiasm." Rahn used the metaphor of a pendulum in another popular speech: "I tell them the pendulum never goes very far but it makes the clock go. A lot of ordinary people just go back and forth to church and work. They never seem to get anywhere but they make the world go."[8]

Rahn did not write out his speeches, instead using short notes because he wanted to have more spontaneity. Although he had many speaking engagements at versammlinge every year, he tried to give different talks, knowing that many in his audience had already heard him speak at another versammling several weeks earlier.

The following excerpt is from a talk given by Clarence Rahn in 1967, transcribed and translated by Ron Treichler.[9] Readers must remember that an oral presentation includes nuances and audience reactions that a transcript cannot convey.

Un sell bringt mich an was ich saage will denowed. Ich hab gedenkt ich deet nemme fer mei Text, "Eselohre." "Eselohre!"

Der Charlie Bortz hot so en Landschtor ghat, un der Riggelwegstation waar baut so en halbmeil vum Schtor weck. Nau wann er ebbes gschickt grickt hot vun der Schtadt, hen sie's abgelaade am Riggelwegstation, un sei Bu iss als nunner fer des Schtoff ruffhohle an der Schtor. Un der Bu hot ee Esel eigschpannt ghat imme Schpringswaage. Un ihr wisst wie Esel sin—sie nemme ihre eegni Zeit. Un mol ee Nummidaag waar en Salesmann uff der Train, un der hot gewaard am Station fer ebber finne fer en nuffnemme ins Schtcddel. Un dann hot er gschwetzt mit dem Bu; no hot er gfroogt eb er mit faahre kennt noch em Schteddel.

"Ya," hot der Yung gsaat, "hock dich yuscht do druff uff em Sitz." Un's waar en heesser Nummidaag, weescht, un sie hen do abgschtert un der Esel hot ewwe sei Zeit genumme. Un der Yung hot so 're Beitsch ghat un er hot em als iwwer

[And that brings me to what I want to say this evening. I thought I would use for my text, "Mule Ears." "Mule Ears!"

Charlie Bortz had a country store, and the railroad station was about a half mile away from the store. Now when he had something sent from the city, they unloaded it at the railroad station and his son would go down to bring this stuff back to the store. And this boy had a mule hitched up to a spring wagon. And you know how mules are—they go at their own pace. And one afternoon a salesman was on the train, and he waited at the station to find someone to take him into town. And then he talked with this boy; then he asked if he could drive along to town.

"Yes," replied the boy, "just sit here on the seat." And it was a hot afternoon, you know, and they started off and the mule took his own time. The youngster had a whip and he used to strike the mule on his ribs, you know, but it didn't accomplish much. Then he hit his backside and again the mule didn't

die Ribbe neigschlaage, weescht, awwer es hot net viel gemeent. No hot er iwwer die Hinnerbacke neigscshlaage un widder net viel gemeent. No widder uff die Ribbe, weescht; no uff em Rickschtrung dronaus.

No saagt der Salesmann, "Ferwass schlaagscht ihn net mol an die Ohre?"

"Ah," secht er, "nevermind. Die Ohre will ich schpaare fer der Hiwwel."

Nau seller Bu waar noch yung, awwer er waar Pennsilfaanisch Deitsch. Er hot sell all gelannt ghat vun Erfaahring, un er hot gewisst wann mer en Esel an die Ohre bissel kitzelt, dann macht er headway.

Ich hab mol so en alder Esel gfaahre; Kitt hen mir ihn gheesse. Un ich hab ordlich speed aus ihn griege kenne. Ich hab im Busch so 're Beitsch abghackt. No hab ich paar Bledder—Laabbledder, weescht—vanne henge losse. Un no hawwich als vorgelangt un hab ihn an die Ohre gekitzelt un no hab ich speed raus ihn grickt. So der Yung hot gelannt wie Dinger zu begreife un wie zu yuuse. Nau mei liewe Freind, sell iss Pennsilfaanisch Deitsch, un ich glaab as sell uns bissel annerschter macht vun viel annere Leit.

react. Then again on the ribs, you know, then on the back.

Then the salesman said, "Why don't you hit him on the ears?"

"Oh," he said, "Never mind. I want to save the ears for the hill."

Now that boy was still young, but he was Pennsylvania Dutch. He learned all of that from experience, and he knew when a mule's ears are tickled, he moves out.

Once I drove such an old mule; we called him Kitt. And I could get pretty much speed out of him. I chopped off a whip in the woods. Then I left a few leaves—foliage— on the front end. Then I reached forward and tickled his front ears, and then I could get speed out of him. So the young boy learned to understand and put things to use. Now my dear friends, that's Pennsylvania Dutch, and I believe that makes us a little different from many other people.]

After telling a series of stories, Rahn turned back to his text.

Brieder Grundsei. Denk mol an seller Yung, weescht, datt uff em Waage mit seinre Heck. Er hot gewisst as Graaft im Esel seine Ohre iss, un er hot der Graaft gschpaart fer der Hiwwel.
    Danki.
	[*Brother Groundhogs, think about that youngster, you know, there on the wagon with his stick. He knew that power was in a mule's ears and he saved the power for the hill.*
	    Thank you.]

Ruth Schaefer, Rahn's daughter, told me that when Rahn was hauling logs in his youth, he learned that mules pulled harder if the driver lightly touched their ears with a branch. His own experiences became the source for his messages.

Don Breininger, currently one of the most popular versammling speakers, acknowledges his debt to Rahn, who was Breininger's wife's pastor and mentored him in becoming a speaker. Rahn advised Breininger to record his talks and then play them afterward so that he could improve his delivery. When Breininger was thinking about moving out of state to take a work-related promotion, Rahn encouraged him to turn the job down in order to continue to remain with the people of the region—something that Rahn himself had done in turning down offers from larger churches in cities. "There was always so much philosophy, true philosophy to retain, and make his speech meaningful even though it was humorous," Breininger told me, adding, "There was so much meaning that could be taken out of it." His preparation for a speech borrows from Rahn. He first looks for a theme or text and then for humorous stories to support it. He does not use extensive notes, preferring the spontaneity of a less structured delivery.

Robert Kline, a retired doctor, is very active in Pennsylvania German heritage activities. He is prominent in groundhog lodges, was president of the Pennsylvania German Society, and served on its board for over fifty years. He also remembers Rahn for his down-to-earth philosophy. He describes Rahn's ability to relate to common people: "As some ministers today, you know, talk about theosophy or some theological stuff and this and

that. Some people don't know what theology is, but there was no problem with Rahn. Rahn talked just like they did. One prayer I remember that he says is, 'behind the bread stands the baker, behind the baker'... and he did so slowly, just like that... 'stands the farmer, behind the farmer stands the miller,' and he went all the way up the chain like this until finally he says, 'and behind the sun and the rain—you are.'"

Paul Kunkel, the leader of another lodge, knew and admired Rahn, and describes his success as a speaker in very similar terms: "The key to Reverend Rahn was the fact that he was a common man. He took common little items that everybody was cognizant of and then embellished it with stories. I remember one session he was talking about the eagle's nest. How the eagle prepares that nest knowing that she has to take care of those young ones, and the preparation that goes into it, and then he embellished it with the stories. You know, those kind of things stick with you."

Richard Miller, a retired college professor of German and an active participant in versammlinge, also emphasizes Rahn's use of a text or message: "He'd use these stories to weave around that text. And he could zero in on that. He was tremendous, he was tremendous. And he always had a good message."

The Reverend Richard Wolf, a retired Lutheran pastor, the former leader of the Berks County Fersommling, and a versammling speaker himself, emphasizes that Rahn's success as a speaker derived from the wealth of his life experiences:

> [Rahn] was able to take from his day-to-day experiences as one who had been raised on a farm, had done farm kind of work, had been a pastor, had been in small towns and sat around the potbellied stoves and had done all those simple things in life where the language was spoken frequently, where the stories were shared about what had gone on in life. All of those kinds of things he could weave into what he was presenting. And his sources were so good. So good.
>
> ... His manner of doing what he did with people was to use the realities of life the way he was experiencing them, to be the basis of the message or the vehicle by which the message was presented to the people.

Rahn's style became the model for a good versammling speech. Clarence Heffendrager, another lodge leader and a popular speaker, describes his own speaking style in similar terms to those described above:

> Well, the first thing I do is . . . my text. The type of speaker I am, I like to tell stories, I like to make people laugh because I think, you know, there isn't a better medicine in the world than a good laugh. So, yes, I tell stories, we can call them off-color stories, but not too off-color. If you ever heard me speak, I control myself so that there is no vulgarity in my speech. But I do like to tell stories and make people laugh but I always keep coming back to my text. I have a text and I speak on that and then I try and fit my stories, but they fit in with that. It is good to laugh and tell stories, but in my opinion you have to give people something to take along home and think about.

Heffendrager told me an example from a lodge speech that he was preparing:

> What I'll be talking about is how back in my younger days, when we were all Pennsylvania Dutch and we had no macadam road and everybody lived on the dirt road. And you lived at the end of the road and you had nothing to worry, nothing to fear, because, you know, nothing was there to bother you. I remember when I was a kid, we never locked the door. We didn't have a key to lock the door. But, as I say, now you live in a different environment, and I live on the main road, and like I say, you put in an alarm system in your house for your protection, which years ago, when we had the dirt roads, you didn't need. Now if you want to call that progress, that's fine with me, and I suppose it is progress. But I also reflect on what we had then and how we lived as opposed to the way situations are today. All around us we have burglaries, all around us, and you know, there are burglaries going on all the time. We didn't have that years ago. We knew everybody, you know. In my younger days I was a contractor—and the little town there that we lived close to, in fact two of them—I knew everybody in town there, I

did their work. Now, I am sorry to say, I don't know my neighbors. You know that has changed.

Starting with the first meeting in 1934 and continuing for many years after, the *Allentown Morning Call* sent reporters to every meeting of Groundhog Lodge #1 and published an extended article about it the following day, including a brief discussion of the theme of the main speech. The use of a "text" to describe some simple but inspirational lessons can be found in most of the speeches. Rahn, as the most popular speaker of his time, is prominent in these newspaper accounts. The following is a sample of the topics from the 1950s to 1970s. In 1956, the Reverend Franklin Silfer talked about making apple butter: "He compared the sweetness of the apples to the good deeds of people, and the constant stirring to the hard work needed to keep these deeds alive." In 1957, the Reverend Clarence Rahn talked about a chicken that laid fifteen eggs, of which only nine hatched. His message was that although not all of our eggs will have chickens, we can still be satisfied with those that do. In 1959, the *Morning Call* described the talks of Rev. Rahn and the Reverend Elmer L. Leisy: "Into the fun they wove some homely but powerful moral lessons." In 1960, Rahn's theme was "Life is like a violin. You must learn to play it, if you want to get the most out of it." In 1964, Rahn brought four horseshoes to the versammling to represent four important Pennsylvania German traits: spunk, judgment, good nature, good management. He explained that without any one of these, a person is like a horse without a shoe—lame. In 1965, Sterling Zimmerman, a very popular speaker who was also mentored by Rahn, told the audience that a team of horses has to be hitched right to pull a wagon, suggesting the importance of teamwork for people as well. In 1966, Rahn used the message that everything has its place, giving the example that a woman's hair is beautiful until cut off: "The man who has money doesn't want his friends to find out he has money and the man without money doesn't want his friends to find out he hasn't any. So the rich man lives poor and the poor man lives rich." He then compared life to going down rows of corn. People should not wait to find the perfect ear and end up with none: "It is a sad thing when we get to the end of our row of corn and find we haven't picked any

cobs." In 1972, Rahn said that the Pennsylvania Germans had always got along with common things and should keep things that way. He then told the story of a man who became wealthy: "since he couldn't write, the man signed checks with two X's. Then the bank noticed he was using three X's to sign his checks. When asked why, he said it was his wife's idea. She felt that since they were now rich, he should have a middle name." At this meeting, there was a noose to hang Punxsutawney Phil for false prophecy (see figure 3), and Rahn was quoted as saying, "it is easy to find pleasure in common things and the proof is in the fersommling that we are now enjoying."[10]

Deitsch as an Expressive Language

These speeches are not only about *what* is said but also *how* it is said. The Pennsylvania German language is often described as being more expressive than English, and many tell me that the jokes in Deitsch do not make as much sense when translated into English. Don Breininger explains the advantages of Deitsch: "I feel very uncomfortable presenting it in English. The stories that we use, the illustrations, they lose their full meaning, they lose their humor in translation. That is what is a shame that they are losing the Pennsylvania German language; it is so colorful. It is so expressive."

One of the few things that Rahn wrote for publication was an introductory note to a dictionary. There Rahn expressed his feelings about the Pennsylvania German language:

> We see now the dialect is a product of Pennsylvania. It has a virility, a richness and charm that it seems to have absorbed from the people and the natural environment in which it grew. A sturdy folk amongst rugged hills, fertile fields, and beautiful valleys could not do otherwise than create a culture such as the Pennsylvanians have produced.
> . . . The dialect makes direct expression possible, and it often takes a whole paragraph in English to express the meaning of one word in the dialect. Pennsylvania German words show a disregard for frills, as did the people who created them. The words of the dialect also possess wonderful powers of description. They served as vessels for the whole faith and life of a fine people.[11]

In addition to the expressive power of Deitsch, speakers often refer to the social contexts in which it was used. Many of the best speakers had experience in public settings, such as hotels, bars, auctions, small stores, and businesses, where people congregated and talked. Rahn himself worked at many different trades as a young man and used these experiences to develop his speaking style. In this respect, the comparison with Mark Twain has special validity. Bernard DeVoto, a scholar of history and the American West, showed that Twain's great contribution to literature was to take the experience of oral legends and spoken stories and make them into literature. Twain gave literature a certain authenticity that was grounded in ordinary experience. Rahn did the same with his talks.[12]

Carl Snyder, the leader of both Lodge #1 and the Grossdaadi Lodge, describes the origins of the speaking style: "Back years ago, people used to congregate at the hotels. That was the social hall, you could say. Men did. And they would have a drink or something, or play cards, because there were no other activities around. I remember down here in New Tripoli they had the whole porch lined up with rocking chairs. And the guys were sitting down there, telling stories, sitting on the rocking chairs, smoking cigars."

Clarence Heffendrager describes the experiences that shaped his development as a speaker: "The most stories I ever heard—Dad did automotive repairs—old-timers would come to Dad's. I remember as a little shaver on up I would sit down in the garage, and these guys would come to have their cars fixed, and my dad and these old-timers would swap stories, and that's where I got a lot of my, you know, input for my storytelling."

Don Breininger recalls that when he was a child, his grandmother was known for being a storyteller in the Deitsch language, and that later he worked at auctions, where he constantly heard Deitsch spoken. He says that he was also influenced by conversations at a local hotel with a tavern: "When we lived in Werleys Corner, I spent a lot of time down at the hotel. And you just weren't sitting at a hotel with a bunch of drunks. That was not what a country hotel was about. It was a kind of social thing. On a Saturday night, the front porch of the hotel, there is a long porch across the front, there is a row of rocking chairs across the entire porch, and the older people sat on the rockers, the younger ones sat on the steps, and we kids would be playing. There was a crowd up there on a Saturday night,

not drinking necessarily. It was socializing, the thing to do." The tavern at Werleys Corner was owned by the family of another very popular speaker, Sterling "Tiny" Zimmerman.

Ruth Schaefer describes a similar background for her father, Clarence Rahn: "He was at his grandfather's, the blacksmith shop, a lot. I guess people came there and stories were told there. And [he] idealized his grandparents. He also would spend some time in Millbach. He had an aunt and uncle that had the hotel and store there."

Expressing Heritage: The American Origins of Deitsch Humor

Mark Twain famously wrote that the art of American humor was in the method of telling the joke, the building of suspense, and the timing.[13] By contrast, a lot of modern humor, for example that found in standup comedy or late night television, is structured around a much faster delivery and rapid punch lines. These modern comedians are very funny, but they present a highly packaged, rehearsed, and, in those senses, manufactured humor. People enjoy the versammling speeches, by contrast, not only for the punch line but also for the style of presentation. The humor of the versammlinge is more drawn out and more connected to a continuing message. While the modern humor of the mass media, like much of the rest of our modern society and lives, has become professionalized and commercialized, the versammlinge preserve an older and more informal type of humor that may be less polished but allows performers to express themselves in spontaneous and personal ways.

The messages often emphasize the strengths of a Pennsylvania German past in which common, ordinary people made unheralded but necessary contributions to daily life. These people also had understanding that often went beyond the elaborate sophistry of those with more formal education. The talks are motivational and inspirational, but, in their emphasis on community and traditional values, they contrast sharply with modern motivational speakers, who focus on personal development, self-actualization, and self-fulfillment. The texts of the versammling messages, by contrast, emphasize values and relationships that are less individual and more grounded in the community.

Richard Wentz, a former professor of religious studies at Penn State and Arizona State, comes from a Pennsylvania German family. He describes the importance of hotels and taverns in the social and verbal life of Pennsylvania Germans in the nineteenth and early twentieth centuries. There is a popular tradition of Pennsylvania German jokes about pastors, or *Parre*, often belittling or satirizing them. Wentz argues that these are examples of the democratization of religion, the jokes bringing the pastor down to the level of the common person.[14] Much of the humor at the versammlinge is a democratic humor that levels the wealthy, the arrogant, and the pretentious. There is a constant emphasis on Pennsylvania German strengths as being derived from their experience as common people in a rural region.

Simon Bronner, a professor at Penn State University and scholar of folklife, has interpreted the earthy and often scatological content of Pennsylvania German humor in psychoanalytical terms, referring to their concerns with cleanliness and order.[15] However, I propose a sociocultural interpretation for the expression of this humor in versammlinge. Farm life is close to nature in all its forms, including animal manure, and the earthy content of Pennsylvania German humor reflects important aspects of that life. Moreover, I think the humor emphasizes and reminds the audience of the earthy roots of Pennsylvania German life. It is another way to highlight the difference between the lives of the common Pennsylvania German and the modern world, where many try to remove themselves from some of the basic elements of ordinary life, including bodily functions.

The humor and messages of the gatherings are derived from a major tradition of American humor that William Blair and Hamlin Lewis Hill trace back to Benjamin Franklin and *Poor Richard's Almanack* and follow through nineteenth-century regional humorists to outstanding practitioners such as Mark Twain, Will Rogers, and politicians such as Harry Truman and Sam Ervin.[16] It is a humor associated with the common person, who is often rural, self-educated, and wise from experience, as opposed to the wealthier person with formal education and often an arrogant manner, who is satirically depicted as acting self-important but ultimately is ignorant in matters of the world. Blair and Hill argue that such humor is based on the concept of the *eiron*, a classical Greek term which

is the root of our word "irony." In Greek plays, the *eiron* was a stock character who displayed a self-deprecatory, simple, modest character but used that to overcome a more privileged and arrogant character. Although this form of humor dates back to classical Greek times and has many European antecedents, Blair and Hill argue that in America it became especially emphasized and elaborated in the comic archetype of the raw rustic who outsmarts the urbane sophisticate and the country rube who overcomes the city slicker, often presented in a drawn-out style, adding to the humor. The practitioners of such humor, Blair and Hill write,

> would all perpetuate what is surely the most dependable American joke—the one based upon the way educated people miss the truth by using book learning while humble, unlearned people find truth by using their horse sense.[17]
>
> ... Even though many raw materials and methods of American humor were universal, by the 1830's it had been decisively molded by the national character. The exaggeration, the anti-intellectual bias, and the interest in native characters and their modulations of the spoken language came together during the antebellum years in ways that would characterize much of our humor for a century.[18]

These are the same themes discussed in the last chapter as displayed in versammling theatricality and identified by Rourke as central in nineteenth-century American popular theater and life. Historian Bernard DeVoto recognized that the roots of Twain's writing were in the storytelling traditions of the American backwoods. In language that emphasizes the same themes discussed by Blair and Hill, DeVoto states, "It is a literature of oral anecdote, whose purpose is the embodiment of character and the revelation of a point, whose aim is the entertainment of listeners, and whose origin is the life immediately at hand. The literature exists for drama, for humor, and for satire. It is the frontier examining itself, recording itself, and entertaining itself. It is the native literature of America."[19] DeVoto also writes about the literary influences on Mark Twain in terms that apply to the lodge meetings: "Through the three decades of the common man following 1828, this literature reached its height. It was

enormously male—emphatic, coarse, vivid, violent, uproarious. A great part of it, too, was bawdy."[20]

The humor at the versammlinge also reflects the humor of Deitsch writers. Deitsch developed as a literary language after the Civil War, and most Deitsch literature falls into two major genres: nostalgic poetry and local color humor, often written for newspaper columns. This latter humor was influenced by the regional "local color" writers, who had roots in the humorous traditions described by Rourke, Blair and Hill, and DeVoto and were popular throughout America in the nineteenth century. Mark Twain's early writings were both influenced by and influential in shaping this national literature.[21] Lee Bressler, discussing the Deitsch dialect literature of the late nineteenth and early twentieth centuries, writes, "The democratic spirit shown in the choice of subject matter, the informality of tone, and the form and method are reminiscent of nineteenth century American humorists."[22] Dialect writers wrote stories that were "sprinkled with homely bits of philosophy."[23]

After the Civil War, regional writing and the use of regional dialects became a way to unite Americans across their many differences. We were all similar in having regional differences, and regional literature allowed all Americans access to these differences. A tension existed between the regional and national, between recognition of local traditions and an attempt to incorporate these traditions into a national project. There was a democratization of American speech that challenged the elitist control over forms of talk, and it fit well with versammling activities. The message was one of democratization and the common person, at the same time that it must also be recognized that the use of Deitsch limited the audience rather than reaching a national one. The Pennsylvania Germans in their literature and in their versammlinge were using broadly American thematic styles to show that they were the same as and also different from other Americans.[24]

Versammling humor is closer to the humor of the nineteenth century and Twain's earlier writing than to Twain's later writing, which became more cynical and despairing, foreshadowing a major current in modern American humor. In the twentieth century, especially after World War I, American humor turned in a darker, more pessimistic and alienated direction that continues to the present. According to Blair and Hill, Twain "was

one of the first nineteenth-century Americans to feel and reflect in his last writings that sense of hopelessness, impotence, and rage which has been dubbed the 'modern malaise.' And in proportions that were unusual for his times, he experimented with some comic (and not so comic) devices for expressing his sense of helplessness—devices which have become the staples of contemporary humor."[25] Although the versammling humor often includes satire and a skeptical view of both the past and present, it is far more hopeful than much of modern humor in its praise of Pennsylvania German life and presentation of a redeeming message or "text."

Silly or Serious: "Sensible Nonsense"

The earthy humor and messages of versammlinge have their critics, including some Pennsylvania Germans. Edwin Fogel, a professor at the University of Pennsylvania and the author of several scholarly works on Pennsylvania German proverbs and folk beliefs, gave a talk at the first groundhog lodge meeting in 1934, in which he summarized the history and traditions surrounding the Christian holiday of Candlemas, which takes place on February 2.[26] Fogel, however, did not approve of the groundhog as an icon of Pennsylvania German identity:

Eb ich uffheer, mecht ich noch frooge, ferwas as unser Grundsau Lodge so en eelendich Ding, wie en Grundsau geweelt hen far unser Sinnbild. Ich perseenlich gleich der Gedanke net, as mir uns der Grundsau nogenaamt hen, un dass mir uns Briedergrundsei heese. "Grundsau" is juscht der Naame far faul, un faul sin mir Pennsylvanisch Deitsche mol net!	[*Before I finish, I'd still like to ask why our Groundhog Lodge selected such a miserable thing as a groundhog for our symbol. Personally, I don't like the idea that we named ourselves after the groundhog and that we call ourselves brother groundhogs. Groundhog is just a name for laziness and we Pennsylvania Dutch are positively not lazy.*][27]

In addition to the choice of the groundhog, Fogel may also have been offended by some of the less serious aspects of the meetings. Other

academics also had reservations. Preston Barba, a professor of German at Muhlenberg College (many Muhlenberg College graduates remember him for encouraging their interest in Pennsylvania German culture and language), was a member of the original board of the Groundhog Lodge #1 but left after five years. A lodge leader who knew him suggested to me that Barba was probably unhappy with the earthy humor of the meetings. I know an academic who complains that the groundhog lodges do not do enough serious work to preserve the language; a pastor, himself active in versammling events, told me that some of his ordained colleagues disapprove of the versammling humor and his participation in it. Heinz Kloss, a German academic who did extensive studies of the Deitsch language, was also critical of the versammlinge for doing little more "than stage a few hours of jolly fun making."[28] Despite these criticisms, many Pennsylvania German intellectuals and scholars, who are unusual in their level of participation in the common life and common events of the people they study, participate enthusiastically in the versammlinge.

Clarence Rahn was aware that some people found the activities of the lodges to be silly and insignificant. In a speech in 1974 given to Lodge #1 at the time of the Watergate hearings, he noted that some outsiders considered the lodges to be *dummheed* (nonsense). But Rahn pointed out that President Nixon, who was facing possible impeachment as a consequence from the Watergate break-in, might have benefitted from doing some of the supposedly *dummheed* things that Pennsylvania Germans do. Rahn again played on the theme of the seeming rustic who in this case had more integrity and knowledge than the nation's most powerful leader. An 1975 editorial in the *Allentown Morning Call* reported that Rahn called lodge activities *verschtennich dummheeda* and commented, "That is best translated as a night of 'sensible nonsense' which is what Groundhog Day and the Grundsow Lodge are all about."[29]

My view is that the lowly groundhog and the earthy humor are part of an important message concerning the knowledge and experience of the common person in American society. The meetings provide a medium for a message about traditional values that allows the participants to view both past and present with new perspectives. Both the medium and the message are rooted in nineteenth-century American life. Cosmopolitan

and academic critics may criticize versammling activities as silly, parochial, pedestrian, banal, and irrelevant. But the very point is that from the perspective of the versammlinge, the sophistry of these intellectuals does not include much common sense.

In creating a tension between the past and present, between superstition and science, and in ceremonially revering what they don't believe, the versammling participants transcend both the present and past in a very contemporary manner. They can observe the past from the perspective of the present and the present from the past, and laugh at both. They can affirm values that highbrow sophisticates may find to be simplistic or naïve, but these very values question the true wisdom of the sophisticates who disparage them. The very style of presentation, which is grounded in a time before modern media, becomes a medium for presenting a way of life that is appreciated. The spontaneity of the skits, with their earthy, slapstick humor, and the delivery style of the speakers resonate with that older time, when conversations and humor were less packaged and more spontaneous and personal, being expressed on the street and in stores, gatherings, and taverns. What is said and performed about Pennsylvania German heritage is also expressed by how it is said and performed.

1
First meeting of Groundhog Lodge #1 in Allentown, February 2, 1934.

2
Raad (board) of Groundhog Lodge #2 watching a groundhog, ca. 1950. Courtesy Clarence Heffendrager, Groundhog Lodge #2.

3
Ferbinnerei (Verbinnerei), oath of membership, Groundhog Lodge #1, 1972. The gallows is for hanging Punxsutawney Phil, a rival of the Pennsylvania German groundhog. Photo: *Allentown Morning Call*. All rights reserved.

4
Ferbinnerei (Verbinnerei), oath of membership, Groundhog Lodge
#2, ca. 1955. Courtesy Clarence Heffendrager, Lodge #2.

5
Crowning the groundhog, 1968. Rev. Rahn is standing at left. Photo: *Allentown Morning Call*. All rights reserved.

6
Back cover of program for Groundhog Lodge #1, 1939. This is a frequently reproduced scene at many different versammlinge, and the words are used at the ending of meetings.

7
Rev. Rahn speaking at Groundhog Lodge #2, ca. 1944. Courtesy of Clarence Heffendrager, Lodge #2.

8
Illustration from program for Groundhog Lodge #1, 1942. Hitler's picture is in a pile of manure. This illustration is from a meeting program only a few weeks after Germany's declaration of war on the United States.

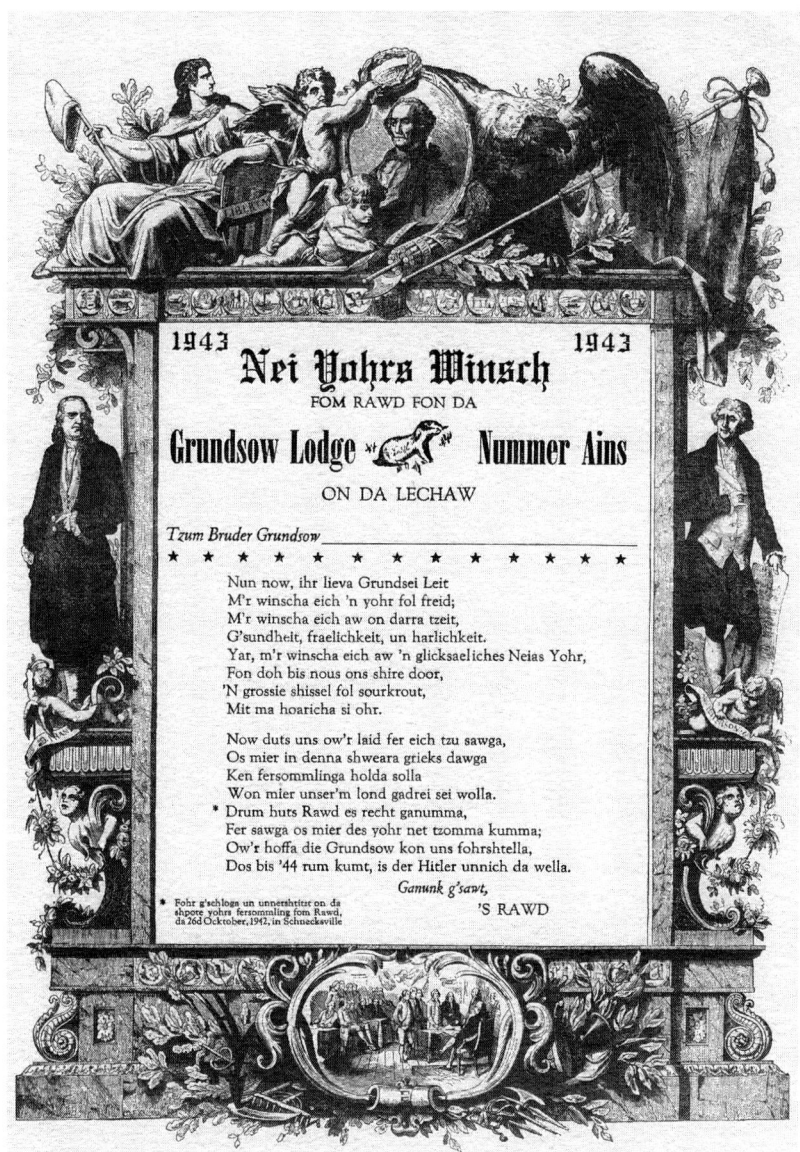

9
New Year's Wish, 1943. Groundhog Lodge #1 suspended meetings during World War II and sent this broadside.

10 (above)
Meeting announcement and invitation for Groundhog Lodge #1, 2011.

11 (middle)
Admission ticket for Groundhog Lodge #1 meeting, 2011.

12 (left)
This *Taufschein* (*Daafschein*), or baptism certificate, commemorates the first organizational meeting of Groundhog Lodge #1 in 1933, and hangs at the front of meetings of Lodge #1. Photo: Dennis Krumanocker.

13
Pennsylvania German flag.

14
Sign hanging at front of meetings of Groundhog Lodge #1: "English Shwetza Is Ferbotta" (Speaking English is forbidden). Groundhog greets participants by saying, "Buva" (boys). Photo: Dennis Krumanocker.

15
Mounted animal scene from the front of the speaker's stand, Groundhog Lodge #1. Rare albino groundhog is on left. Photo: Dennis Krumanocker.

16 (opposite)
Eight-foot-tall groundhog statue that is at the front of every meeting of Groundhog Lodge #1. In past years a person was inside and wheeled the statue into the meeting. Photo: by Dennis Krumanocker.

17
Raad (wheel, board) listing the members of the board of Groundhog Lodge # 1 in 2015. This wheel hangs over the stage at meetings of Lodge #1. Photo: Dennis Krumanocker.

18
View of meeting of Groundhog Lodge #1 at Germansville Fire Company, 2013. Notice groundhog at right and various signs at the front of the stage. Photo: author.

19 (opposite)
"Schnitzelbank" song from the back covers of Lodge #1 programs, this one from 2011.

20
Band at Groundhog Lodge #1, 2015. Photo: Dennis Krumanocker.

21
Procession bringing in a stuffed groundhog to be placed at the podium, Groundhog Lodge #1, 2013. The stuffed groundhog is in a case being carried by men behind the man carrying the flag. Photo: author.

22
The thirteen members of the *Raad* (board) of Groundhog Lodge #1, standing in front of the large groundhog, 2005. Photo: author.

23
Ferbinnerei (Verbinnerei), oath of membership, Lodge #1, 2015. Photo: Dennis Krumanocker.

24 (opposite)
Program cover for Groundhog Lodge #1, 1958. The groundhog is on the moon, perhaps in response to the launch of the Russian Sputnik satellite in 1957.

25
Program cover for Groundhog Lodge #1, 1962. The groundhog cooks a favorite recipe, *Rivla* soup (*Riwwelsupp*), while missiles fly outside the window.

26
Program cover for Groundhog Lodge #1, 1965. The groundhog watches images of summer and winter on television.

27
Program cover for Groundhog Lodge #1, 1970. The groundhog is on the moon, after the American landing in 1969.

Grundsow Lodge Nummer Ains
ON DA LECHAW

Die Drei Un Fotzich'dt
Yairlich Fersommling
uns Fesht

Da Tzwet Harnung, 1979
om halver sivva
Northampton Community Center

28
Program cover for Groundhog Lodge #1, 1979. Wild inflation provides the background for the groundhog in winter and summer scenes.

29
Program cover for Groundhog Lodge #1, 1999. The groundhog, responding to current events, asks President Bill Clinton, "Where is this young woman Monica?"

30 (opposite top)
Rev. Rahn gives the main speech in front of a coffin for the goose, a weather-predicting rival of the groundhog, Groundhog Lodge #1, 1970. Photo: *Allentown Morning Call*. All rights reserved.

31 (opposite below)
Women protest that they cannot attend meetings, Groundhog Lodge #1, 1973. Photo: *Allentown Morning Call*. All rights reserved.

32
Performers at Groundhog Lodge #2, ca. 1965. Courtesy of Clarence Heffendrager, Lodge #2.

33 (opposite top)
Local television crew interviewing Bill Meck, dressed as a groundhog, and Groundhog Lodge #1 leader (*Haaptmann*) Bill Williams, 2013. Photo: author.

34 (opposite below)
Doctor giving an injection during a skit, Groundhog Lodge #1, 2013. Photo: author.

35
Groundhog being brought across the Jordan Creek, Lehigh County, February 2, 2013, as part of the activities of Groundhog Lodge #16. About two hundred people waited on shore for the forecast. Photo: author.

6.

Region and Nation

CONTEXTS FOR THE VERSAMMLING MOVEMENT

Maintaining a distinctive ethnic culture while also participating in the national society is a constant theme in Pennsylvania German life, a process that, following work by historian Steve Nolt, I have termed "ethnic and American." Since their earliest settlements, Pennsylvania Germans have preserved and developed a distinctive ethnicity and way of life. At the same time, they have participated in American society and incorporated many American practices into their daily lives, even using these practices to maintain their distinctive ethnicity. Versammlinge display theatrical, literary, humorous, and rhetorical traditions that have roots in American popular culture. The versammlinge also developed during the 1930s in a national context of increasing appreciation for the regional, preindustrial, traditional practices of ordinary people, often associated with "folk" culture, and national events that celebrated these regional cultural traditions and the lives of common people. These national developments resonated with developments in Pennsylvania German regions. Collectors and museums began accumulating the artifacts and materials of everyday Pennsylvania German life. The leaders of versammlinge and heritage

events had roots deep in Pennsylvania German culture and expressed the views of the common folk in the formation of these events. Pennsylvania German scholars were also closely involved in heritage activities, not only recording and analyzing the culture but, to an unusual degree for academics, participating in the events that they described.

Making Pennsylvania German Ethnic Identity

Henry Harbaugh (1817–1867) is often viewed as the exemplar of the nineteenth-century Pennsylvania German who is both Pennsylvania German and also very American, and his life is a forerunner to the themes that are central in the versammlinge. Pennsylvania German religious scholar Richard Wentz describes Harbaugh as the "quintessential Dutchman," and Nolt sees him as the key figure in the development of a Pennsylvania German ethnic identity in the middle of the nineteenth century.[1]

In working his way to prominence, Harbaugh was an ordained minister in the German Reformed Church and became a professor at that denomination's theological school in Mercersburg in south-central Pennsylvania. But he always stressed his humble origins, which were reflected in his very literal understanding of the Bible, salvation, and heaven, conservative even by the standards of other contemporary theologians, who were developing more abstract and interpretive views of heaven and salvation.[2] Harbaugh represents the Pennsylvania German tradition of being both a patriotic American and a strong supporter of Pennsylvania German heritage. Although deeply influenced by his Pennsylvania German origins, he supported national values and patriotism. During the Civil War, he was a firm supporter of Abraham Lincoln and the Northern cause, although many Pennsylvania Germans, largely Democratic in their political affiliations, were far more ambivalent about the war. Harbaugh expressed his views about religion, the nation, and his heritage in the *Guardian*, a religious journal targeting young people that he edited for the German Reformed Church. In this journal he included patriotic poems and essays extolling general American values as well as Pennsylvania German culture and heritage. He also published poems he had written in the Deitsch language. After his death, some of these poems were combined into a volume,

Harbaugh's Harfe, which became very popular among Pennsylvania Germans. Although there had been sporadic attempts to write in Deitsch before, scholars trace the development of Deitsch as a literary language to Henry Harbaugh.[3]

Nathan Schaeffer, an eminent Pennsylvania German who was state superintendent of public instruction in Pennsylvania, remembered seeing Harbaugh in 1866 at Franklin and Marshall College in Lancaster (at the time an important college for German Reformed students). Schaeffer was a student at a commencement address, and Harbaugh was called upon to make a toast. The audience at Franklin and Marshall were mostly Pennsylvania Germans who had academic backgrounds and were fluent in both Deitsch and English. Schaeffer describes Harbaugh's entry and toast:

> When the toast was announced, he attracted attention by walking forward in the manner of an old farmer, pulling off a slouch hat with both hands, and catching a red bandanna handkerchief as it dropped from his forehead. His first sentence,
>
> "Es gebt gar greislich gelerente Leut, und Ich bin awe aner dafun," ("*There are some very learned people, and I am one of 'em,*")
>
> sent a flash of merriment through the assemblage. When he proceeded to enumerate the learned languages—
>
> "Es gebt sieve gelehrte Sproche: Englisch und Deutsch, Lateinisch und Griechish und Hebraeisch; sell sin fünf. Die sechst haest Pennsylvania Deutsch, die sievet is German Reformed,"— ("*There are seven learned languages, English and German, Latin and Greek and Hebrew; these are five. The sixth is called Pennsylvania German, the seventh is German Reformed,*"—[)]
>
> there were shouts of laughter over the entire hall.[4]

The humble arrival, the use of the Deitsch language, which, though loved, was probably not ordinarily considered appropriate for a scholarly

setting, the inclusion of Deitsch as equal to Greek and Latin, and finally the inclusion of the German Reformed religion, the religion of most of those present, as a "learned" language, illustrates the combination of humor, modesty, and pride that is often at the core of versammling humor. Harbaugh was playing a humorous version of the *eiron*, the person who appears to be unsophisticated but in fact is well educated in common sense and understands the common people. In doing so, he praises the people and their language and religion. Harbaugh was proud of his nation, and also proud of his Pennsylvania German heritage: he was earthy, humble, and humorous. These became essential features of Pennsylvania German ethnic identity for the next 150 years, and many of the versammling events take inspiration from them.[5]

Harbaugh's poetry in the *Guardian* started a literary movement that became a major vehicle for the expression of Pennsylvania German culture and heritage. In the late nineteenth and early twentieth centuries, there were books of poetry, plays, and newspaper columns written in the Deitsch "dialect." Deitsch literature falls broadly into two genres. The first, mentioned in the previous chapter, is earthy, humorous columns that combine homespun philosophy with colorful depictions of Pennsylvania German life. Thomas Harter, who was the guest of honor at the first versammling in Selinsgrove in 1933, is often considered the preeminent writer in this tradition. William Troxell, as Pumpernickle Bill, was another very popular columnist in this style. The second genre, which developed directly from Harbaugh's poetry, was poetry eulogizing rural life and times, often set a generation earlier than it was written.[6] Both genres often express related themes of a simple life surrounded and eroded by a changing world that has become more commercial, materialistic, impersonal, and industrial, and both themes are important at the versammlinge.

Harbaugh died in 1867. But his life and work expressed values that would become important for Pennsylvania Germans after the Civil War as they became more self-conscious in developing events to express their ethnic identity and heritage. Many people, both scholars and laypeople, both from within and outside Pennsylvania German life, began to describe, catalogue, collect, display, and praise Pennsylvania German accomplishments and lives. In 1876, as part of the national celebrations

of the centennial of the Declaration of Independence, Pennsylvania German educators commemorated their contributions to public education in Pennsylvania with a monument in Kutztown featuring inscriptions in Standard German, Latin, English, and Deitsch. The monument is an early example not only of the use of written Deitsch in any context but also of the connection of the language to a patriotic event.[7] During this time, leading Pennsylvania German educators advocated bilingual programs that supported the use of Deitsch. In 1875, Abraham Reeser Horne, the principal at Keystone State Normal School (now Kutztown University), published a book in Deitsch, *Pennsylvania German Manual* (the first edition was entitled '*M Horn sei Pensilfawnish Deitsh Buch* [Horne's Pennsylvania Deitsch book]), that was intended to help students learn to read and write in Deitsch and also included passages in Deitsch about Pennsylvania German traditions and famous Pennsylvania Germans to develop pride in the heritage. Horne was an early proponent of bilingual education, proposing that Pennsylvania German children learn to read and write in both Deitsch and English. The Kutztown University library has a copybook from 1876 that contains the results of an examination in Deitsch, presumably given to the normal school's students who were learning to write, and perhaps teach, in that language. In 1876, Samuel Baer, a leading Pennsylvania German educator, argued for a view of Pennsylvania Germans that was neither based on their Germanic origins nor on the dominant national population whose ancestors came from the British Isles. In a report to the state's superintendent of public instruction, he wrote, "We are neither Germans nor Englishmen, but Americans."[8]

There were many other ethnic and heritage events. In 1893, teachers in Berks County organized a special day to honor Conrad Weiser, an early Pennsylvania German settler and leader. Money was raised to erect a monument for Weiser in 1909, and in 1928, twenty-five thousand people attended a dedication ceremony for the Conrad Weiser Memorial Park.[9] In 1900, Philip C. Croll (1852–1949), a Lutheran pastor, founded a journal, the *Pennsylvania-German*. For the next five years, under Croll's editorship, the journal published Deitsch poetry, historical articles, and biographies of famous Pennsylvania Germans.[10]

Reflecting this rising ethnic self-awareness, a group of leading Pennsylvania Germans gathered in 1891 to establish a scholarly ancestral society, the Pennsylvania German Society, intended to praise and describe the accomplishments of the Pennsylvania Germans. The society was part of a trend in the late nineteenth century to assert ancestral connections to immigrants who came in the colonial period. Societies such as the Sons of the American Revolution, the Daughters of the American Revolution, the General Society of Mayflower Descendants, and the Society of Colonial Wars, among many others, were all founded about the same time. The founders of the Pennsylvania German Society insisted that full members of the society be able to demonstrate ancestral connections to eighteenth-century immigrants from the German regions of Europe. Many of the society's early members were concerned that their heritage and their ancestors' accomplishments were being distorted by historians from other regions of the nation, especially New England, who belittled or ignored Pennsylvania Germans. They were especially concerned because these historians were writing the textbooks that were being taught to Pennsylvania German children in schools.[11]

The Pennsylvania German Society has a long and excellent record of scholarly publication. It has published more than most regional, county, and state historical societies, and even many national academic and scholarly societies. The society has published an annual volume almost every year since 1891 (in addition to the twenty annual volumes published by the Pennsylvania German Folklore Society before the two societies merged), a journal that has been published regularly since 1967, and many special publications. Moreover, most of the work is not simple hagiography of ancestral accomplishments, although this was important to the founders of the society. The publications include many first-rate descriptions of Pennsylvania German lives, culture, language, history, and crafts.

Collecting Heritage and Praising the Lives of the Common Folk

The development of Pennsylvania German heritage and ethnic events at the turn of the century was part of a strong interest throughout the nation in the preindustrial lives of ordinary Americans. Collectors and

museums began paying attention to the craft traditions and material culture of the eighteenth and early nineteenth centuries, including those of the Pennsylvania Germans.

Henry Mercer (1856–1930), although not a Pennsylvania German himself, is a major figure in the collection and display of Pennsylvania German material culture. Independently wealthy and academically trained as an archeologist, Mercer was one of the very first to systematically collect the material culture of everyday life, such as door latches, locks, cooking utensils, apple presses, construction tools, kitchenware, house furnishings, stoves, and roofing materials, among many others (his collection includes a gallows). Mercer, as an archeologist, reasoned that he would preserve the material before it was thrown away and left for archeologists of future millennia to excavate. He collected these items of everyday life from a few generations earlier that were no longer being used but had not been discarded. He collected near his Bucks County home, including in Pennsylvania German areas. The Mercer Museum, which he established and is now managed by the Bucks County Historical Society in Doylestown, has the most important collection of eighteenth- and nineteenth-century material culture in the region, and perhaps the entire country. Mercer also wrote several books that called attention to the folk and craft traditions of eighteenth-century Pennsylvania Germans, including the illuminated manuscript writing style that is now known as *Fraktur* and the biblical imagery molded into the side plates of Pennsylvania German stoves.[12]

In 1903, Edwin Atlee Barber (1851–1916), curator of ceramics at the Pennsylvania Museum and School of Industrial Art (as it was then known), wrote a book about the redware pottery tradition of Pennsylvania Germans.[13] Redware was brought from Germany in the eighteenth century and flourished in the second half of the eighteenth century into the early nineteenth century. It was mostly replaced by imported and manufactured ceramics by the middle of the nineteenth century. Barber was one of the first to notice the redware tradition as something worth valuing and collecting.[14]

During this time, two Pennsylvania German brothers from Lancaster County, Henry Kinzer Landis (1865–1955) and his brother George (1867–1954), began collecting everyday farming and household tools, often

buying them at auctions, and displaying them in their farm museum, the Landis Valley Museum, which was eventually taken over by the State of Pennsylvania and is now administered by the Pennsylvania Historical and Museum Commission.

Pride in the expression of Pennsylvania German culture experienced a hiatus during World War I. Although Pennsylvania Germans had no allegiance toward the German nation, anything Germanic was viewed with distrust in American society, and many Pennsylvania Germans felt that their loyalty was being questioned and that they were under increased scrutiny. The Pennsylvania German Society suspended its meetings from November 2, 1916, until October 8, 1920.[15]

The late 1920s into the early 1930s, however, saw revived enthusiasm for Pennsylvania German culture. The revival came as part of broader developments in American society, including an emphasis on regional lifestyles, the interest of Americans in preindustrial folk culture, a national trend to idealize preindustrial life, and, during the 1930s, an emerging New Deal emphasis on the "common" people. Enthusiasm for Pennsylvania German culture came from the outside in the form of tourists and wealthy collectors, and from Pennsylvania Germans themselves, who continued to redefine themselves in a variety of events both as American and as a group with distinctive experiences and history.

The collections of Mercer and the Landis brothers initially had a regional audience. But with increasing intensity after World War I, Pennsylvania German material culture acquired a national audience, as exemplified by two major exhibitions. Joseph Downs, a curator at the Philadelphia Museum of Art, worked with the wealthy collector Henry Francis du Pont to present an exhibition of Pennsylvania German material culture and decorative arts at the museum in 1929. The exhibition included the inside of an eighteenth-century kitchen, built in traditional German style, from a house in Millbach, Lebanon County, as well as furniture and household items (the exhibit is still in the Philadelphia Museum of Art). In 1934, Downs organized an exhibition of Pennsylvania German materials at the Metropolitan Museum in New York City. The acclaim received by these two exhibitions brought large numbers of outsiders to appreciate Pennsylvania German accomplishments and instilled a new sense of pride among Pennsylvania Germans themselves.[16]

SERIOUS NONSENSE

Travel books appeared that romanticized Pennsylvania German life for a popular audience. Travel writer Wallace Nutting described Pennsylvania Germans in his 1924 *Pennsylvania Beautiful*, and his interpretation of the large designs on barns as "hex signs" painted to keep witches away intrigued people from outside the region and also set off an acrimonious dispute about the meanings of these signs that continues to this day. Nutting was an outsider, but another writer, Cornelius Weygandt, had Pennsylvania German ancestors and roots in Pennsylvania German experience. In 1929, Weygandt, a professor at the University of Pennsylvania, wrote a travel book about the Pennsylvania Germans, *The Red Hills*, that became very popular. Other books about Pennsylvania German history, crafts, and folk customs became popular in the 1930s, both among Pennsylvania Germans and others.[17] This attention from outsiders contributed to the pride that Pennsylvania Germans felt in their culture and heritage. The interest in regional lifestyles from both within the region and outside inspired the founding of the Pennsylvania German Folklore Society, which held its first general meeting on May 4, 1935. The society became another important source for the publication of scholarship about Pennsylvania German life.[18]

The widespread public fascination with Pennsylvania German culture was enhanced by its distinctiveness in a rapidly industrializing society and its proximity to the major urban centers of Philadelphia, New York, and Baltimore. The increased use of the automobile in the 1920s and 1930s made the area more accessible to outsiders and also made interactions and meetings of Pennsylvania Germans amongst themselves much easier.

Don Yoder refers to the 1920s and 1930s as a time of revival in Pennsylvania German culture. He describes three main approaches that shaped Pennsylvania German interactions with the larger American society. The approaches correspond to the three languages of Pennsylvania Germans: Standard German, English, and Deitsch. "Germanizers" wanted to emphasize and maintain the German roots of Pennsylvania Germans. The more numerous "Americanizers" wanted to emphasize assimilation into the larger society. Finally, "dialectizers" wanted to preserve and express themselves through the Deitsch language.[19] Many Pennsylvania Germans combined varying degrees of all these approaches. There has always been a strong tendency among Pennsylvania Germans toward

Americanization and far less interest in Germanizing. The dialectizers were strongly patriotic and American in their orientation, but they were also proud of their heritage and wanted to express it through events and activities, especially in the Deitsch language. It was the dialectizers who led this revival and inspired the versammling movement and other Deitsch events.

The Versammlinge and Deitsch-Language Events

As part of the Pennsylvania German cultural revival, the 1920s and 1930s saw a flowering of Deitsch-language events. According to Homer Rosenberger, "In the early 1920s there probably was a yearning among many Pennsylvania Germans for the dialect columns and other writing in the dialect that had faded into the background during World War I."[20] In 1928, Clarence Iobst wrote a short play in Deitsch, *En Quart Millich un en Halb Beint Raahm*, that was performed at Emmaus High School, outside of Allentown. The humorous plot involved a husband mistakenly suspecting his wife of having an affair with the milkman. All ends well as the misunderstandings are cleared and love prevails. The play was a smash hit in the area, and it was presented in many other locations. It also inspired many other Pennsylvania German plays and contests in the Allentown area in the late 1930s.[21]

Pennsylvania Germans also began to hold Deitsch-language church services. In the eighteenth century and well into the nineteenth century, many church services were held in Standard German, although it must be assumed that sermons included more Deitsch as the nineteenth century progressed and the American-born preachers moved further away from Standard German. After the Civil War, increasing numbers of churches switched to English, and by World War I there were only occasional Standard German services. Deitsch was rarely if ever used as a language for sermons. By the 1940s, however, although English remained the main language in churches, there were special church ceremonies in Deitsch, usually periodic or annual events, which were performed as heritage events. These continue to the present.[22] Pennsylvania Germans also began to hold "liar's contests," in which contestants competed to tell the

biggest lie in Deitsch. These events became very popular. The "tall tale" is often considered a very American form of oral expression, and this is another example of how Deitsch-language events had roots in American experience.[23]

New technology was used to express the Deitsch language. In 1937, Gilbert Snyder, known as "Die Wunnernaas," started a radio show in Deitsch that ran until his death in 1956, with an estimated 250–300,000 listeners in 1942.[24] William Troxell also had a very popular Deitsch radio show.[25]

In 1935, Preston Barba, a professor of German at Muhlenberg College, began a weekly column, 'S Pennsylfawnisch Deitsch Eck (The Pennsylvania German/Dutch corner), in Allentown's main newspaper, the *Allentown Morning Call*. Publishing material in both English and Deitsch, the column ran for over thirty years, until April 5, 1969, and became a very important source for materials in Deitsch and about Pennsylvania German culture more generally.[26]

Three Leaders in the Expression of Pennsylvania German Heritage: William Troxell, Thomas Brendle, and Clarence Rahn

Many people were important in the revival of Pennsylvania German culture in the 1930s. But in my research three men stood out in terms of their energy, enthusiasm, and impact: William Troxell, Thomas Brendle, and Clarence Rahn. These three led the revival of Pennsylvania German culture through the middle of the twentieth century, and their accomplishments continue to influence Pennsylvania Germans to the present. They had deep roots in Pennsylvania German life and developed events to express those roots in a wide range of heritage and cultural activities. They were key people in the development of the versammlinge.

William Troxell, the founder of the groundhog lodges and the leading disseminator of the versammling movement, was born on June 11, 1893, in the small village of Rising Sun in Lehigh County. He graduated from Kutztown State Normal School in 1913 and did some studies at Muhlenberg College. He was a teacher for about five or six years, and then joined the staff of the *Allentown Morning Call* in 1926. He became a Deitsch "dialect"

columnist for the *Morning Call*, writing a popular column several times a week. He also had a radio show in Deitsch.

Troxell organized the first local folk festival, held in Allentown, Pennsylvania, on May 3 and 4, 1935. The Allentown event was a prelude to a statewide festival held at Bucknell University later that year. Troxell put together a play, set fifty years earlier, in which a country gentleman, played by himself, receives guests. The format allowed him to present Pennsylvania German dances, songs, legends, folk beliefs, and games. The following year, Troxell organized another folk festival in Allentown on June 26 and 27. It used essentially the same format with some elaborations. The formal opening of the festival was led by Troxell's close friend and associate Thomas Brendle. The first night had a square dance contest. The next day, a series of presentations described Pennsylvania German life. There were fiddlers who played Pennsylvania German tunes and then separate presentations of children's and adult games. The third night followed the model from the previous year by presenting a play that described Pennsylvania German life, including songs, dances, games, and finally, to represent the end of a person's life, an auction of possessions.[27]

Troxell continued to present events like this both in Allentown and elsewhere, including at the 1940 New York World's Fair, where scenes were presented from a Pennsylvania German farm of "about half a century ago."[28] Troxell also organized Deitsch playwriting contests in Allentown in 1941 and 1942.[29] Troxell, in conjunction with regional granges, presented "Apple Butter Days" at Dorney Park, an amusement park in Allentown. (Granges are fraternal organizations focused on farming. They are similar in their ritual and symbolic activities to the Freemasons and other fraternal organizations, although they include both men and women.) Starting in 1944, this annual event included a variety of Deitsch-language activities and Pennsylvania German presentations.[30]

Troxell's folk presentations were early examples of the cultural displays that became popular throughout the country. National and regional folk festivals usually featured songs and dances. Troxell's did as well, but the dramatic reenactments of Pennsylvania German farm life that he added foreshadowed a movement throughout the nation toward a more comprehensive display of regional and ethnic practices at "folklife" festivals.

Troxell provided some of the inspiration for the Kutztown Pennsylvania Dutch Folk Festival (now the Kutztown Folk Festival), first held in 1950, which, in its depiction of Pennsylvania German folk-cultural practices, became a model for many other folklife festivals in the nation, including the Smithsonian Folklife Festival.[31]

In addition to his newspaper columns, Troxell edited an anthology of translations of well-known English literary works into Deitsch, *Aus Pennsylfawnia* (Out of Pennsylvania); published examples of traditional Pennsylvania German New Year's Wishes, *Alta Neiyohrs-Winscha* (Old New Year's wishes); assembled, with Thomas Brendle, a collection of Pennsylvania German folk songs as part of a book of Pennsylvania folk songs; and edited and translated, again with Brendle, *Pennsylvania German Folk Tales, Legends, Once-Upon-a-Time Stories, Maxims, and Sayings*.[32] Troxell was president of the Pennsylvania German Society from 1952 until his death on August 10, 1957, at sixty-four.

Deitsch-column writer, speaker, and performer, Troxell created cultural events at the same time that he was celebrating a cultural tradition. From versammlinge to folklife festivals, he was the preeminent organizer of events that celebrated Pennsylvania German culture and activities. In the very act of presenting the culture to others, these events preserved the culture. They made cultural preservation and heritage something that was not simply an obligation, but fun and enjoyable.

The Reverend Thomas Royce Brendle was another central figure in the versammling movement and the expression of Pennsylvania German culture and heritage. Brendle was a very close associate of Troxell. Brendle's daughter, Helen Milroy, remembers that Troxell and Brendle talked almost daily and that Troxell was a frequent visitor to her household. The two collaborated on many projects, including publications, folk presentations, Deitsch events, and versammlinge, and both served on the board of the Pennsylvania German Society. Brendle was born in Schaefferstown, Pennsylvania, on September 15, 1889. He entered Albright College in 1904. After three years there, he went to Franklin and Marshall College, graduating in 1908. He graduated from the German Reformed Church's seminary in Lancaster in 1911 and was ordained as a Reformed pastor. Brendle was first called to minister in Abilene, Texas, where he stayed for two years.

His daughter says that he recalled those years as being frustrating because he was unable to increase the numbers in his ministry. In 1913, he returned to Pennsylvania and was installed as the pastor of the Old Goschenhoppen charge of the Perkiomen Valley. During World War I, he also helped out as a schoolteacher, since the war had caused a shortage of teachers. In 1926, he took over the Egypt charge (which included churches in Egypt, Laurys, and Cementon) near Allentown. He served there for thirty-five years until his retirement in 1961. After his retirement, he moved to New York to be near family members, and finally moved back to Allentown, where he resided at the time of his death on September 1, 1966.[33]

With Troxell, Brendle was closely involved in the state folk festivals in Allentown and at Bucknell University, and the two were on the original board of Groundhog Lodge #1. He wrote the play for the first groundhog lodge meeting in 1934. Brendle was a strong advocate for and participant in Pennsylvania German events, many of which were developed by Troxell. Brendle's contributions, however, were more academic and scholarly than Troxell's. In 1936, Brendle began to keep a comprehensive set of notes about Pennsylvania German customs. Many of these notes he collected while doing his rounds as a pastor, or during daily life among Pennsylvania Germans, going to the market, walking on the street, going to meeting places. Other notes were recollections of events or customs from his youth growing up in Schaefferstown. The notes eventually grew into more than fifty-five thousand entries about Pennsylvania German folklife, contained in ninety-three notebooks.[34] C. Richard Beam, a leading authority on the Deitsch language and former professor of German at Millersville University, edited some of Brendle's notebooks and writes, "In the last quarter of the twentieth century the ranks of those who know the dialect well and recall the old ways are thinning rapidly. It would no longer be possible to replicate Brendle's solitary achievement. His folklore collection is his monument. He truly was 'the dean of PG [Pennsylvania German] folklorists.'"[35]

Long before he began keeping these notes, Brendle had been collecting folk-cultural material. His earliest notable publication about Pennsylvania German folk culture was *Plant Names and Plant Lore Among the Pennsylvania Germans* (1923), coauthored with David E. Lick. He also published "Folk

Medicine of the Pennsylvania Germans: The Non-occult Cures" (1935), coauthored with Claude W. Unger. Published by the Pennsylvania German Society, the two books include significant information about Pennsylvania German folklife that would soon have been lost. *Plant Names and Plant Lore* is a comprehensive guide not only to nomenclature but also to how plants were used for a variety of purposes, including medicinal, ceremonial, and culinary. It was written at a time when information was available from people who still used plants for food, medicine, and household needs. *Folk Medicine* is a comprehensive, detailed source on the home remedies that people still used or remembered using before the widespread introduction of modern medicines.[36]

Brendle wrote several Pennsylvania German plays. In addition to the skit he wrote for the first groundhog lodge meeting in 1934, he wrote *Die Mutter* (The mother), which was first performed at the 1934 meeting of the Pennsylvania German Society, and later *Die Hoffning* (The hope). *Die Mutter* and *Die Hoffning* are unusual for Deitsch plays in that they are not comedies, but dramatic performances with serious content.[37]

Brendle also wrote a biography, "Moses Dissinger, Evangelist and Patriot" (1959). Dissinger was a Pennsylvania German who became a popular preacher for the Evangelical Association (which was derived from the Methodist teachings of John Wesley, with a special focus on Pennsylvania Germans). Dissinger was notable for his earthy, direct, confrontational approach to preaching, in which he often emphasized his simple origins. Dissinger is often seen as exemplifying someone who used the experience of his common Pennsylvania German "Dutchy" background to become an influential preacher, mixing humor with everyday examples, as seen in the lives of Henry Harbaugh in the nineteenth century and Clarence Rahn in the twentieth century.[38]

Clarence Rahn was discussed earlier as the preeminent speaker at versammlinge. His life experiences not only provided the material for his versammling speeches, but extended to impact other areas of Pennsylvania German culture and heritage. Rahn was a renaissance Deitsch man and in my view the twentieth-century equivalent of his fellow Reformed minister Henry Harbaugh. He was born July 17, 1898, in Temple, Berks County, near the city of Reading. He attended a one-room school for eight years

and then took the trolley to attend Kutztown State Normal School for five years, graduating in 1918. His daughter says that this was a common way to complete a high school education at the time. He continued his education at Schuylkill Seminary (which was not a religious seminary and eventually merged with Albright College in 1929). During World War I, he taught for a short time in Allentown near an army camp. He was preparing to go to officer training school, but the Armistice was signed before he started. According to his daughter, during the war he became concerned about warfare and pursued a career in the ministry after deciding that "the only thing that was going to keep peace in the world was Jesus Christ." He was raised as a Lutheran, but decided that the German Reformed theology was closer to his personal religious philosophy and went to a Reformed seminary, Lancaster Theological Seminary, graduating in 1923. Before his graduation he had already started as a temporary "supply" minister at the Jacksonville charge, a group of "union" churches in rural areas of Berks and Lehigh Counties. Union churches were very common when Pennsylvania Germans first settled this region and had limited resources. Lutheran and Reformed congregations would share a church building, although they often kept separate congregations and held separate services. As communities prospered and the population increased, most of these union congregations divided into separate Lutheran and Reformed congregations and built separate churches, but a few union churches continued into the twentieth century, and some still remain at present. Rahn always supported the maintenance of the union churches. During Rahn's ministry the Jacksonville charge grew to include five churches. Rahn stayed with the charge for fifty-two years. Although he was offered larger, more prestigious, and better-paying ministries, he never wanted to leave this group of churches because of the obligations and ties he felt to the congregations.

Rahn was a key performer in Pennsylvania German culture during the twentieth century, and he was especially important in the versammling movement. He kept an extremely active schedule as a speaker at Pennsylvania German events. He was also a speaker in English at many meetings, including service clubs, conventions, and other events. According to his daughter, Rahn's original motivation for public speaking

was financial. During the Great Depression, the chicken farm he operated with a relative failed, leaving him in debt. To pay the debt, as he promised he would do, he began to take every speaking engagement that was offered to him.

Rahn also wrote the scripts for the very popular Deitsch radio program *Asseba un Sabina* from early 1944 until the show went off the air on June 27, 1954.[39] The weekly show was structured around humorous views of various situations in the lives of a Pennsylvania German farm couple. Many people recall stopping whatever they were doing on Sundays to listen. The scripts were also performed before live audiences at public events. Dr. Robert Kline, a lodge leader, recalls that there were "wall-to-wall people" at these events.

It is remarkable that Rahn could create a script for the show every week for ten years.[40] William Fetterman, an authority on Pennsylvania German folk theater, describes the content of the show:

> Rahn took over the writing of the series [following the death of Lloyd Moll, who wrote the first five scripts in early 1944] because he realized the need for such a thing within the culture. The radio program was a convenient and accessible medium through which to depict his experiences in the Pennsylvania German community—the humor, the philosophy, and the love found there. He understood the common people, and was able to portray them with humor *and* dignity.
>
> *Asseba un Sabina*'s success was due to a magical combination of good acting and good material, and that material was very much a product of Rahn's fertile imagination.[41]

In a thesis about the radio plays, Zach Langley sees them as a culmination of the Deitsch-language movement, which formed a Pennsylvania German folk identity and stretches from the Deitsch-literature writers of the nineteenth century to the versammlinge of the twentieth and twenty-first centuries.[42]

Rahn had a widely varied life that provided many of the themes and humor in his talks. In his youth, he worked in a stone quarry, on a road crew, in his grandfather's blacksmith shop, and he drove a steamroller.

Later, he ran a chicken farm and taught school. He also operated an informal consulting business to advise churches on raising money. He was good with his hands. He made wooden bowls and patented a pipe that he sold through mail order advertising. He designed and built a barbeque grill before they were mass produced and marketed in stores. He also was electronically inclined, building radios in the early days of that medium, then moving to more advanced recording systems as the technology was developed. He used his knowledge of technology to record many of his own talks. On top of all this, his daughter Ruth remembers that he was an accomplished cook and was especially good at baking bread.

On Friday, February 4, 1977, Rahn gave a talk to Groundhog Lodge #11. His text was that we should talk about people before their funeral the same way that we talk about them at their funeral. On his way home from the talk, he suffered a heart attack. He died the following Tuesday, February 8.[43]

Rahn himself has become part of the folklore of people in the region. Many people remember him, and I frequently find that when his name comes up in a conversation, someone has a story they heard from him. After I mentioned him at one talk, a woman came up to me with a story he told. While giving a sermon, he noticed a woman who had a cold and kept wiping her nose with her right sleeve. After the service, as was very common in the area, this woman asked Rahn if he would like to come to her house for dinner. Rahn replied, "Well, that depends upon which hand you cook with." At a recent conference, there was a speech about *Asseba un Sabina*. Afterward, someone from the audience stood up to illustrate Rahn's humble sense of humor by retelling a story he heard from him. A pastor was invited to dinner by a wealthy farmer. After the meal, the farmer asked the pastor to come for a drive to see the farmer's land. The farmer proudly pointed out different large parcels that he owned: "I own that land, and that over there, and that one." After the farmer finished showing all the land, he looked to the pastor for a comment. The pastor looked impressed and replied, "That is really a lot of land," and, after a pause, added, "I wonder who will own that land in a hundred years." Russell Heintzelman, a retired Reformed pastor, knows my interest in Rahn and told me the following story he heard from him. A church congregation,

eager to expand its buildings, wanted to buy a plot of land from a neighboring farm. After several years the farmer was ready to sell his farm. The church offered to buy a parcel that was next to the church, but not the rest of the land. The farmer refused, saying that he wanted to sell the entire farm, not just a parcel. He complained that the church only wanted the good land, but if they wanted to buy his land, they had to take it all, good and bad. Rahn took this as the source for a "text": if you want what is good in life, you also have to take things that are not so good.

Rahn's conversion from the Lutheran to the Reformed Church is noteworthy. Both Reformed and Lutheran ministers are important in events that express Pennsylvania German ethnicity. Although they represent a smaller denomination, it seems to me that the Reformed ministers are more active in these events. Don Yoder has also found that German Reformed ministers have been more involved than the leaders of other denominations in creating a Pennsylvania German ethnic identity. Yoder suggests that the Reformed Church was undergoing increased factionalism after the Civil War and that the development of a shared Pennsylvania German ethnic identity unified them.[44] Another possible reason is that Reformed Church services are less liturgical and the pastors are often more egalitarian and down-to-earth, while Lutheran services are more formal and "high church." The perspective of a Reformed minister is closer to that of a common, ordinary, earthy person. Rahn's son-in-law, Richard Schaefer, was a Lutheran pastor and deeply admired his father-in-law. He agreed that Rahn's earthy appeal was more in line with the orientation of the Reformed Church. Schaefer described the Lutheran Church as more "formal," telling me that "Lutherans at that time were strongly liturgically oriented."

Troxell, Brendle, and Rahn found ways to praise the accomplishments of common people. Troxell was the leading organizer of Pennsylvania German events, founding groundhog lodges, spreading all varieties of versammlinge, organizing folk festival presentations, and writing a Deitsch column in the *Allentown Morning Call*. Brendle was the most academic of the three, writing several scholarly books and keeping a treasure trove of notes about Pennsylvania German folklife. Rahn wrote little in scholarly journals, one publication being a collection of humorous Deitsch stories

with English translations.⁴⁵ But he had an immense impact on the oral culture of Deitsch during the twentieth century by speaking at versammlinge, participating in liars' contests, and writing radio skits. All three men had roots in rural life, all related to people in a direct way, all were involved in the daily lives of Pennsylvania Germans, and all were involved in the events that celebrated Pennsylvania German heritage and identity.

Studying and Participating: Scholarship of and by Pennsylvania Germans

The celebration of the common person is also evident in much of the scholarship about Pennsylvania Germans. When I first started learning about Pennsylvania Germans, I was somewhat skeptical about the scholarship. Much of it was being done by people who were Pennsylvania German themselves and participated in Pennsylvania German activities. I expected more detachment and distance, less focus on the people themselves and more attempts to integrate material about them into a broader scholarly discourse about ethnicity and modernization. Over time, however, I began to admire how much Pennsylvania German scholars participated in the life they described. Partly my changing views came from my becoming increasingly tired, as I grew older and left my time in graduate school further behind, of social theories and interpretations that seemed more and more abstract and detached from common experience. And partly they reflected change in the field of anthropology, with greater emphasis being placed on letting people speak for themselves, expressing themselves in their own voices, rather than having their culture described by some outsider with an academic background.

The development of Pennsylvania German heritage activities is notable because of the degree to which scholars with Pennsylvania German backgrounds have participated in them. By contrast, although there is considerable national scholarly interest in the Old Order groups, especially the Old Order Amish, almost all of the research on them has been done by scholars who have left the groups or come from outside, often from more culturally liberal Anabaptist groups. But Pennsylvania German scholars of the Church people usually come from the culture they are writing about and enthusiastically participate in many of its activities, including

the versammlinge, folklife festivals, and other heritage events. They are scholars of cultural practices who actively participate in those practices, and they often present their research in formats accessible to ordinary Pennsylvania Germans. Preston Barba had a Ph.D. from Yale and taught at Muhlenberg College. In 1935, he started a weekly column in the *Allentown Morning Call,* 'S Pennsylfawnisch Deitsch Eck, that appealed to people from all backgrounds and social classes and was loved for thirty years by the *Morning Call*'s Pennsylvania German readership. Harry Hess Reichard had a Ph.D. from Johns Hopkins University and also taught at Muhlenberg College. He played Asseba in Clarence Rahn's popular radio show *Asseba un Sabina* and participated in versammlinge and folk festival presentations. Alfred Shoemaker had a Ph.D. from the University of Illinois. He started a weekly paper in 1949, the *Pennsylvania Dutchman,* which was widely read in the region, more by laypeople than scholars, with as many as 12,500 subscribers. In 1950, in an effort to have common Pennsylvania Germans present their daily lives and activities to a broader public, Shoemaker established the Kutztown Pennsylvania Dutch Folk Festival. In his endeavors, both as editor and festival organizer, Shoemaker collaborated with Don Yoder, a scholar with a Ph.D. from the University of Chicago, who went on to achieve national prominence as a folklore and folklife expert but also maintained close contacts with ordinary Pennsylvania Germans. Albert Buffington had a Ph.D. in German from Harvard, was a professor at Penn State University and later at Arizona State University, and was a first-rate linguist. He broadcast a weekly radio program in Pennsylvania German from Sunbury, Pennsylvania, as the *Nixnutz* (troublemaker), a Deitsch term used to describe mischievous children. Lay scholars with limited formal academic training also made important contributions to Pennsylvania German publications, including those of the Pennsylvania German Society, the *Pennsylvania Dutchman,* and its successor, *Pennsylvania Folklife.* Lay scholars also had leading roles in heritage events, such as the Landis brothers with their farm museum and Troxell, Brendle, and Rahn, among others, with a wide range of publications, presentations, and events.

    In a discussion of the academic development of the concept of "tradition," Simon Bronner notes that some leading Pennsylvania German scholars, notably Alfred Shoemaker and Don Yoder, have argued that folklore

and the study of tradition should be locally grounded in the ethnographic study of specific communities. Bronner suggests that Pennsylvania, since the time of William Penn, has been supportive of localized cultural and religious differences. Elsewhere he argues that by the middle of the twentieth century there was a "new class" of academics who wanted to place a greater emphasis on studying diverse and sometimes marginal ethnic groups and acting as brokers between these groups and the larger society.[46] Pennsylvania German scholars were certainly part of this new class, but they had unusually deep roots in their own culture and unusually close involvement with the heritage events representing and praising that culture.

The Common Folk in National Culture: American Contexts for Pennsylvania German Heritage

The versammlinge developed in a period of heightened national interest in regional life and folk culture. In a discussion of how Americans celebrate and remember their past, cultural historian Michael Kammen describes a public and intellectual fascination with the common person and folk culture that swept all segments of American society in the 1920s and 1930s.[47] This fascination was expressed across a wide range of cultural events. As discussed earlier, in popular culture and mass media, Will Rogers represented the common person and enjoyed great popularity as a performer, writer, radio host, and movie star. In academic studies, Constance Rourke wrote a groundbreaking study of the folk roots of American humor in 1931, describing the figures and genres in nineteenth-century American popular humor and drama.[48] In 1932, Bernard DeVoto published his findings on the sources for the writings of Mark Twain. Refuting the literary and psychoanalytic interpretations of Twain that were dominant at the time, DeVoto pointed to the important role of newspaper stories, storytelling, and folk tales in Twain's life experiences that shaped his writings.[49] The emphasis on common lives extended to literature, art, and other expressive forms. George Gershwin composed his opera *Porgy and Bess* in 1935. Aaron Copland composed *Billy the Kid* (1938), *Rodeo* (1942), and *Fanfare for the Common Man* (1942). Thomas Hart Benton and Grant Wood developed

stylized paintings in a "regionalist" style that praised common activities and common people. Writers like John Steinbeck and James Agee worked a related territory in literature. Even the wealthiest elites were praising the common people. There were very aggressive efforts by America's wealthiest families, including the Fords, Rockefellers, and du Ponts, to collect and display American regional folk culture in their museums.

The earliest annual "folk festivals" were organized at this time, including the Mountain Dance and Folk Festival in Asheville, North Carolina, in 1928; the White Top Folk Festival in Grayson County, Virginia, in 1931; and the National Folk Festival in Saint Louis, Missouri, in 1934. Troxell and others were involved in several of these early national festivals, in addition to those held in Pennsylvania. The developing interest in folk festivals during the 1930s is reflected in the appearance of that term in the historical indices of the *New York Times*. I found 6 references to the term "folk festival" from 1895–1923; 1 in 1929; then 2 in 1930; and 2 in 1931. After that there is a sudden burst: 53 in 1932; 38 in 1933; 28 in 1934; 45 in 1935; 53 in 1936. Across the decades, the indices show 3 uses of the term from 1920 to 1929; then 394 from 1930 to 1939. World War II created something of a hiatus, as the number drops to 144 from 1940 to 49; then it recovers, with 234 from 1950 to 1959, and 548 occurrences from 1960 to 1969. The most recent full decade, 2000–2009, shows 209 occurrences, lower than in the 1930s. Most of these uses appear to be occasions when different ethnic groups or national groups performed songs and dances, although as early as the 1930s Pennsylvania Germans were including cultural performances, such as plays, craft presentations, and reenactments of everyday life, in many of their performances and displays.[50]

Two of the principal organizers of the groundhog lodges, William Troxell (Pumpernickel Bill) and the Reverend Thomas Brendle, explained their own interest in collecting folk materials as partly inspired by the new interest in regional folklore: "A revival of popular interest in Pennsylvania German folklore, and particularly in our folk songs, resulted from the meetings of the Pennsylvania Folk Festival at Allentown in 1935 and at Bucknell University in 1936 and 1937 under the direction of George Korson, and those of the Pennsylvania German Folk Festival at Allentown, 1936–1941, under the direction of William S. Troxell."[51]

The versammlinge developed from both broader influences in American culture and the long-term efforts of Pennsylvania Germans to express their heritage and ethnicity. In the 1920s and 1930s, there was a synergy of forces that provided the context for the development of the versammlinge, and a revival of efforts to express Pennsylvania German ethnicity and heritage that had been limited in the years immediately following a war with Germany. There was also a national interest in regional cultures that further encouraged Pennsylvania Germans to express themselves in a variety of activities. These activities continue today as the major expressions of Pennsylvania German heritage in folklife festivals, in heritage organizations, events, and displays, and in Deitsch-language events, including special church services, liars' contests, and versammlinge.

7.

The Future of Pennsylvania Germans and Their Versammlinge

Tradition concerns the past, but the celebration of tradition in heritage events is constantly changing as time turns new experiences into past experiences and as people reassess their pasts from new vantage points. Heritage changes and evolves, and heritage events about traditions can themselves become traditional. The versammlinge, which started as a way to celebrate Pennsylvania German heritage and ethnicity, became over time part of that heritage and ethnicity.

The activities at the versammlinge became ritualized, following a similar format every year. A high degree of theatricality and ceremony is involved, especially in the groundhog lodges: pledging loyalty to the lodge and the groundhog, listening to a weather report, singing patriotic songs in Deitsch, and ending every meeting by asking God to allow them to keep their way of life and their merriment. Within this repetition, however, there is continual creativity, as current events are incorporated into the versammling performances, speeches, and skits.

As part of my research for this project, I read old microfilms from the *Allentown Morning Call* about the activities of Lodge #1 since the early

1930s. Every year there were upbeat articles about the groundhog lodge's activities, and it struck me that next to these articles, there was news about some of the most challenging events in American history. The versammlinge started during the height of the Great Depression. World War II followed, then the Korean War, the Cold War, the Civil Rights Movement, the tumult of the 1960s and the Vietnam War. Much of my research was done in the time soon after the attacks on the World Trade Center in 2001. It is not that the members of Lodge #1 ignored these events. They suffered through the Depression, many are veterans, and they continue to struggle with adverse economic and security problems like everyone else. Nevertheless, in the midst of difficult times, they took time to turn to something that was removed from daily troubles and mostly for enjoyment. The groundhog provided a temporary foil for the challenging events and changes that were very much a part of their lives, and also a perspective for contrasting the past and present. Their heritage did indeed transcend difficult times, which were lived through and somehow overcome, and the meetings continued.

The lives of the Church Pennsylvania Germans have changed since the formation of the versammlinge in the 1930s. In the midst of a postindustrial society, they have lost many of the cultural practices that are relayed across generations informally by word of mouth, observation, and shared daily life and are associated with a culturally distinct group of people. There are still some regional distinctions that are widely maintained in intonation patterns, in a few linguistic phrases, and in celebrations like eating *Fasnachts* (a potato dough specialty) on Shrove Tuesday or eating pork and sauerkraut on New Year's Day. Most of the distinctive regional folk practices, however, were discontinued or replaced by the last quarter of the twentieth century. The founders of the versammling movement were raised in the late nineteenth and early twentieth centuries and experienced much of this regional folk culture and the Deitsch language. So, to a degree, did many of the consultants and informants for this book. These people, in their seventies and eighties when I interviewed them in the first decade of the twenty-first century, remembered a time when Deitsch was spoken on street corners and in stores and homes. Many of the activities of the versammlinge hark back to this rural life. But this past frame of reference, at least as ingrained in personal experience, is constantly moving forward as older generations pass

on and younger generations remember back to their youth. Today, Deitsch is rarely spoken, even in homes. In sixty or seventy years, the children of today may have nostalgic memories of their youth, but those memories will not include a Deitsch-speaking community, a largely rural economy, and many Pennsylvania German folk practices. They may hold a vague memory of a grandfather who went to meetings where people spoke only in Deitsch. In this changing cultural context, events that celebrate a past culture become the most tangible expressions of that past culture.

The performance styles of the versammlinge encourage a high level of individual participation and expression. Compared with humorous traditions that developed later in the twentieth century, versammling humor depends upon a longer, more drawn out presentation. Usually it is more optimistic than much contemporary humor and often structured around a broader text or message. In celebrating a traditional life, the versammlinge provide a personal means of communication and performance to convey a meaningful message, and, if not always certain about the future, are always positive about patriotism, religion, the common person, and Pennsylvania German heritage.

The versammlinge carry an implicit view about present-day life. This view is not so much a criticism of modern life. Indeed, the people at these meetings participate in modern life, and since most are in their seventies and eighties, I think it is fair to conclude that they made their own contributions to making that life. Rather, the versammlinge create a dialogue, a way to highlight the modern by contrasting it with the past and to remind people about how things are different, whether for better or worse. Thus, we have the common image in skits and stories of the naïve Dutchman who is both ridiculed for his lack of understanding and appreciated for his simple bewilderment at the convolutions of modern life, creating a tension that examines both the past and present.

Many academics who study heritage events in the United States and around the world find that organizers of folk festivals and heritage events, who often come from academic or professional backgrounds, can have different agendas from those of the people who are being represented or who are presenting.[1] The versammlinge and many other Pennsylvania German heritage events are unusual in the degree to which they are managed by

people who are both the organizers and the presenters of a culture. The versammling movement has its roots in the enthusiasm of the Pennsylvania Germans themselves. The versammlinge are unlike most other heritage organizations, including museums and festivals, which are clearly established to make money, even if they are organized as nonprofits, and often ask for funds from public and private sponsors to subsidize their work. In contrast, the versammlinge are self-supporting, noncommercial, and have never asked for any grants or support. Many American holidays and festive occasions, such as Easter, Valentine's Day, and Mother's Day, were developed by commercial interests into opportunities to make money, but commercialization is not part of the Groundhog Day celebrations of the Pennsylvania Germans.[2]

Many in academia also criticize heritage events for staging or distorting a past to serve the interests of the present. While many heritage events try to camouflage their staging and reconstructions, the versammling staging is explicit, especially in the groundhog lodges, which combine pseudo-Masonic ritual with groundhog ceremonials. The explicit staging creates an ironic distance that contrasts and assesses both the past and the present. Few, if any, are seriously claiming that the groundhog predicts the future, or that they are accurately performing Masonic rituals, or that the caricatures in the skits are real people. Nevertheless, within this staging some real concerns are presented. Modern-day cynics will criticize the values presented in the speeches as simplistic and naïve, but I find something refreshing in the presentations' aphorisms and straightforward simplicity. The events allow people to participate in fellowship while praising the accomplishments of their ancestors, preserving earlier forms of personal interaction and communication, examining both their past and their present, and expressing values that are important, all in the language of their ancestors and their youth.

Versammlinge and the Futures of Pennsylvania Germans

The future of the versammling movement is uncertain. Most participants are in their seventies, eighties, and nineties, and every year there are fewer people at the gatherings. So far, all the groundhog lodges, except for the

one at Temple University, continue to meet.[3] But attendance is down at most versammlinge. It is very rare for anyone in the Church groups born after 1940 to have much ability in Deitsch. Although the groundhog lodges sponsor Deitsch-language classes, very few graduates attain the fluency needed to follow the versammlinge, and it seems unlikely that they will be able to replace the continuing loss of older speakers.

Some suggest that the gatherings include more use of English to attract more people, and there are lodges that have done so. Many people, however, feel that if they use English they will lose their unique identity and the rhetorical power of the Deitsch language. Deitsch, moreover, is often presented as the language of the common, ordinary person, which, coupled with its expressive power, makes it an important part of the ceremony. The humor may not resonate as deeply or meaningfully in English. Others suggest that women be admitted to the groundhog lodges. But this might result in losing some men, and, as pointed out above, the general versammlinge that include both men and women are also losing members, and many have been discontinued.

It is always difficult to predict what will happen to languages that are losing speakers and becoming marginalized. A recent survey from around the world suggests that there are many different paths in language maintenance and loss. Often languages show surprising resilience and revitalize themselves. Usually this is the result of concerted educational and governmental support or when marginal peoples associate resistance to a dominant group with resistance to the dominant group's language, and revive their language as part of this resistance. Neither is the case for Deitsch speakers.[4]

It is hard to imagine how the versammlinge can continue in their present form for another generation. My own view is that a few will continue as Deitsch-language events, a few will become English-language events, some will mix the two languages (as is already happening), and many will be discontinued. I am more optimistic about Pennsylvania German culture, which has found many ways to be expressed over the past three hundred years. A myriad of festivals, heritage events, and regional historical societies will continue as locations for the expression of Pennsylvania German ethnic identity. Probably some Deitsch-language events will be maintained, although with far fewer participants.

For most present-day Pennsylvania Germans, their traditional folk and cultural practices are not integral to all the contexts of their lives, as they might have been a hundred years ago. Church Pennsylvania Germans still participate in a secular ethnic identity in a celebratory manner through events that were developed in the late nineteenth and twentieth centuries, including versammlinge, historical reenactments, folk festivals, and other heritage events. They keep household possessions, handed down from ancestors, or purchased more recently at auction, or as reproductions, to represent a Pennsylvania German aspect of their identity. Pennsylvania Germans are much more self-conscious now as they think about what it means to be "Pennsylvania German," or remember how different life was when they were young and they had grandparents who spoke Deitsch, or consider the stories about past times told to them by their elders. Just as Pennsylvania German culture and ethnic identity changed between 1700 and 1800, and again by 1900, so too it is different today.[5]

In this modern, perhaps postmodern, world, I do not think that there is necessarily any one future for Pennsylvania German culture or heritage. Rather, there are multiple futures with different forms of expression for different people, and most likely a continual transformation of both culture and heritage, as there has been in the past. Some will continue at the versammlinge; others may continue at modified versammlinge; still others, without knowledge of Deitsch, may take part in a variety of different heritage events. Some will continue to celebrate holidays in a certain way, eating pork and sauerkraut at New Year's or *Fasnachts* on Shrove Tuesday, or cooking a family recipe. Some will tell family stories that have been handed down. Some will read books about Pennsylvania German culture or take classes at heritage centers or colleges. Some will take a special interest in traditional crafts and practices such as *Fraktur*, redware, long rifles, barn stars, and folklife festivals. Some will participate in many or all of these activities.[6]

For many in the early twenty-first century, ethnicity has become less about what is done in everyday life and more about self-identity and participation in specific, often ceremonial, activities. Pennsylvania German identity is part of a long heritage, a sense of identity in contrast with other ethnic groups, a source of pride for the past accomplishments of

Pennsylvania Germans, and a source of guidance for some core values, derived from these accomplishments, about how to live. But it is no longer a way of life that permeates everyday activities as it did in the late nineteenth century and into the beginning of the twentieth. It is something that becomes represented in special events and activities. For some, this may represent the demise of Pennsylvania German culture. From another perspective, it may also reflect the modern expression of ethnicity in the twenty-first century. For those living in a differentiated, specialized, postindustrial society, it is hard to see how ethnic identity could be any other way. The participants in versammlinge are involved in many different activities and relationships in many different settings. One man is a retired road worker, auctioneer, avid hunter, clown in the Philadelphia Mummers Parade, and presenter at Pennsylvania German events. Another is an engineer, a graduate of a leading research university, a volunteer at retirement homes, a Freemason, an active participant in heritage events, and a teacher at Deitsch-language schools, among many other activities. Such a variety of careers is typical of many participants. The versammlinge are one part of modern, complex, multidimensional lives, events where people express an important part of their lives and where they can also assess their modern roles and identities.

Pennsylvania German events emphasize the many contributions that Pennsylvania Germans have made to American society, including in the arts, technology, science, printing, and even holiday celebrations such as Christmas and Easter. Perhaps another important Pennsylvania German contribution is their development of events and organizations to celebrate their heritage. After the Civil War, the Pennsylvania Germans explored new literary forms to celebrate their heritage and developed organizations such as the Pennsylvania German Society to describe their culture. After World War I, new events developed, including folk presentations, displays of material culture, and various language events, including the versammlinge, all of which continue to the present. Pennsylvania Germans will likely continue to construct new ways to express themselves in the future. Whatever the future holds, they have shown how an ethnic group can participate in and incorporate elements from a larger society to maintain their distinctive heritage and identity.

Notes

Preface

1. There is a website for my research on Sikaiana, http://www.sikaianaarchives.com.
2. For some results of this research, see Donner, "Assimilation and Localism."
3. See Donner, "'Neither Germans nor Englishmen, but Americans'"; Donner, "'We Are What We Make of Ourselves.'"
4. For discussions about Belsnickle, see Shoemaker, Yoder, and Weaver, *Christmas in Pennsylvania*; for powwowing, see Hohman and Donmoyer, *Der Freund in der Noth*. The folk festival in Kutztown has undergone several name changes. For the purposes of this book, I will refer to it as the "Kutztown Folk Festival," although its founders originally called it the "Kutztown Pennsylvania Dutch Folk Festival," and for a time it was called the "Kutztown Pennsylvania German Festival," and more recently, the "Kutztown Folk Festival."

Introduction

1. Pennsylvania Germans usually distinguish among the different types of meetings by referring to the groundhog lodges as *Grundsow Lodge/Grundsau(sei) Lodsch(e)* and the general versammlinge as *versammlinge/fersommlinge*. But each annual meeting of a groundhog lodge is called a *versammling/fersommling*. While in programs and materials the spelling is usually *fersommling/e*, I will use *versammling/e*, the spelling that is preferred by scholars of the language, for reasons explained in chapter 1. I will also follow their precedent by using the singular *versammling* as an adjective: thus, the development of many *versammlinge* led to the *versammling* movement.
2. See *Allentown Morning Call*, February 1, 1975, 6. I am indebted to Clarence Rahn's daughter, Ruth Schaefer, for making available a tape recording of Rahn's talk entitled "Sensible Nonsense," given at Deer Lake, Pennsylvania, on April 19, 1975.
3. The language will be discussed in chapter 1.
4. Among the Church (Lutheran and German Reformed) people, I have never encountered anyone who was not a fluent speaker of English. Occasionally, I meet someone who remembers an older relative from their youth who did not speak English.

Chapter 1

1. In a forthcoming book, *Pennsylvania Dutch: The Story of an American Language*, Mark Louden, a professor at the University of Wisconsin and a leading scholar of the Pennsylvania German language, argues on scholarly grounds for the use of "Dutch" as opposed to "Pennsylvania German." William Woys Weaver, a scholar of the people's foodways, also recently made a strong case for the use of "Dutch." See Weaver, *As American as Shoofly Pie*. See also Yoder, "Palatine, Hessian, German," for a discussion of terminology and culture.
2. Kammen, *Mystic Chords of Memory*; Lord, "'Patriotism and Piety'"; Swank, "From Dumb Dutch to Folk Heroes."
3. For general introductions to Pennsylvania Germans, see Yoder, *Discovering American Folklife*; Wood, *Pennsylvania Germans*; Parsons, *Pennsylvania Dutch*; Rosenberger, *Pennsylvania Germans, 1891–1965*. For a discussion of early settlement, see Fogleman, *Hopeful Journeys*; for a discussion of settlements in the nineteenth century, see Donner, "Research Note." In addition to Anabaptists, the "Sect" people are often described as including Schwenkfelders and Moravians. In my experience, Schwenkfelders and Moravians are very similar in their daily lives to the "Church" people. These categories are somewhat loose, and although many Pennsylvania Germans are Lutheran, Reformed, Schwenkfelder, or Moravian, not all members of these denominations consider themselves to be Pennsylvania German. The German Reformed denomination has gone through several mergers. The most notable took place in 1957, when it joined with the Congregational denomination to form the United Church of Christ. I will continue to refer to this denomination as "German Reformed" because I think that term describes the history and orientation of the membership as described in this book.
4. For some recent discussions of the Old Order groups, see Kraybill and Nolt, *Amish Enterprise*; Kraybill, *Riddle of Amish Culture*; Kraybill and Bowman, *On the Backroad to Heaven*; Kraybill and Hurd, *Horse-and-Buggy Mennonites*. I use the term "conservative" to refer to the Anabaptist groups that resist many new cultural and technological practices. Patrick Donmoyer has correctly pointed out to me that many Church Pennsylvania Germans who use the most modern technology consider themselves to be "conservative" in a political and religious sense. The use of terms like "liberal" and "conservative" can be complicated. I attended a seminar in which a Catholic academic pointed out that in his youth he was taught that Anabaptist teachings of the sixteenth century were "radical."
5. In the nineteenth century, Germantown was incorporated into the city of Philadelphia.
6. See Yoder, "Reformed Church." Yoder makes the same point that

Anabaptists have a stronger religious identity than a secular ethnic identity.

7. See Buffington, *Similarities and Dissimilarities*. I first saw this use of the term "Deitsch" in an article by Zach Langley, "*Asseba un Sabina*: The Culmination," and I am following his usage here.

8. I am indebted to Mark Louden, Ed Quinter, and Gregory Hanson for discussing the implications of the terms "Standard German" and "High German." Among people in the region there is a common tendency to refer to Deitsch as "the dialect." Jennifer Schlegel (personal communication) found that people taking adult classes to learn Deitsch referred to these classes as "dialect classes."

9. For the demise of the German-language press, see Waldenrath, "German Language Newspress"; for a general discussion of the political and historical contexts for Deitsch, see Kloss, *American Bilingual Tradition*, especially chaps. 2 and 5. I have discussed these issues in relation to education; Donner, "'Neither Germans nor Englishmen, but Americans.'" For an excellent overview of the Deitsch language, see Louden, "Development of Pennsylvania German Linguistics." Again, a comprehensive and detailed discussion of the language will be found in Professor Louden's forthcoming book, *Pennsylvania Dutch*.

10. My colleague Jennifer Schlegel pointed out to me that the origin of this adage can be traced to statements at an event attended by the famous linguist Max Weinrich; see https://en.wikipedia.org/wiki/A_language_is_a_dialect_with_an_army_and_navy/.

11. See Buffington and Barba, *Pennsylvania German Grammar*; Beam, Brown, and Trout, *Comprehensive Pennsylvania German Dictionary*. See also Louden, *Pennsylvania Dutch* (forthcoming).

12. The problem is compounded because the typographers of Deitsch written materials often misplace letters (switching *i* and *e* is common); in one notable example, the term *Liever* (*Liewer*, dear) in a very common prayer is misspelled as *Leiver* in numerous programs. I have used E. Stine, *Pennsylvania German Dictionary*, Lambert, *Pennsylvania-German Dialect*, and Beam, Brown, and Trout, *Comprehensive Pennsylvania German Dictionary*, as guides for spelling, but have always kept the sources' original spelling system in transcriptions.

13. See, for example, Kemp, *Pennsylvania German Versammlinge*. Despite his use of *versammling* in publications, Kemp was one of the founders of the Berks County Fersommling.

14. Giddens, *Consequences of Modernity*; for a discussion of drama in harvesting games, see Fetterman, "Mosch Riehre"; for a general discussion of the changes in this region, see Donner, "Assimilation and Localism"; for a discussion of related issues of culture change in a midsized city in Indiana in the 1920s, see Lynd and Lynd, *Middletown*, especially pt. IV, 225–312; for a discussion of changing media and forms of personal expression

on Sikaiana, see Donner, "Don't Shoot the Guitar Player." In my article "Assimilation and Localism," I examine how modernization has changed towns in this region and the ways in which people try to maintain some of degree of local identity and interpersonal relationships. The article addresses these issues in the late twentieth century and was written before I did research on the versammlinge.

15. See Smith, *Cultural Heritage*; for a recent discussion of heritage events in Pennsylvania, see Kitch, *Pennsylvania in Public Memory*. In my research in the Solomon Islands, I found the past was contrasted with the present in such a way that the present could be understood better; see Donner, "*Kastom* and Modernisation on Sikaiana"; Donner, "Same Old Song but with a Different Meaning.'"

16. Donner, "Reply to Boyer." For an interesting analysis of the many ways in which a heritage event can be used and understood, see Bruner, *Cultures on Tour*, especially 145–68. For discussions of the staging and manipulation of heritage, see ibid.; Kirshenblatt-Gimblett, *Destination Culture*; Comaroff and Comaroff, *Ethnicity, Inc.*

17. For a discussion of the charity schools, see Weber, *Charity School Movement*. For an insightful discussion of Franklin's ambivalent relations with Pennsylvania Germans, see Frantz, "Franklin and the Pennsylvania Germans." Mark Louden (personal communication) points out that part of Franklin's prejudice toward Pennsylvania Germans stemmed from the Anabaptist refusal to fight in any wars. Much of the Quaker population remained pacifists as well.

18. Nolt, *Foreigners in Their Own Land*.
19. Kazal, *Becoming Old Stock*.

Chapter 2

1. Miller, *Pennsylvania German Groundhog Lodges*.
2. Mark Louden (personal communication) has suggested to me that Pennsylvania Germans may have overemphasized the degree of anti-German feeling that they experienced in World War I. This is certainly a possibility, but there was some dampening of Pennsylvania German activity during and following World War I. The people I talked with, children of the people who lived during the war, all said their parents remembered that there was a lot of prejudice toward all German Americans, including Pennsylvania Germans.
3. This regional and national context will be discussed at greater length in chapter 6.
4. Kemp, *Pennsylvania German Versammlinge*, 195, 197.
5. Edward Quinter (personal communication) tells me that there is a common winter festival celebrated in Germany, Winter Austreibungsfest (Driving away the Winter Fest). Since there were scholars of Standard German involved with the versammling, it is possible that there was some relationship in meaning.

6. *Selinsgrove Times*, March 16, 1933, 7.
7. Harter, *Boonastiel*; Buffington, "Pennsylvania German Prose and Poetry"; Musser, "Life and Work of Thomas H. Harter"; see also Reichard, *Pennsylvania-German Dialect Writings*, 203–9.
8. In the nineteenth century, regional or local color writers used local characters with regional dialects to describe regional customs, often with humor and satire. These writers included Artemus Ward, Josh Billings, and the early Mark Twain, among many others.
9. *Selinsgrove Times*, March 16, 1933, 1, 7. This type of humor continues to the present. Following Obama's election in 2008, Groundhog Lodge #1 had a skit in which the president phoned the meeting and spoke in Deitsch about his Pennsylvania German ancestry.
10. Troxell, "First Grundsow Lodge," 4.
11. *Selinsgrove Times*, January 23, 1937.
12. Yoder, *Pennsylvania German Broadside*, 159–61.
13. There is no position similar to county superintendent at present. Kemp oversaw public schools throughout the county. Today these duties are divided among eighteen separate district superintendents.
14. Kemp, *Pennsylvania German Versammlinge*, 199.
15. Ibid., 218. Note that Kemp uses "Dutch" to describe the meal, but "Pennsylvania German" for everything else.
16. The *Allentown Morning Call* records some of Troxell's activities in spreading knowledge about the meetings, including a talk at the University of Pennsylvania in 1944: *Allentown Morning Call*, February 2, 1937, 20; February 2, 1937, 5; February 3, 1944, 5.
17. The origins of the lodges are found in Troxell, "First Grundsow Lodge." The number 13 has special symbolic significance for Freemasons. There were many Freemasons involved in the development of the groundhog lodges, and much of the content of these meetings is borrowed from Masonic practices. Among other meanings, the number 13 can refer to the Last Supper, where there were thirteen present, Jesus and the twelve disciples.
18. Lehigh County Historical Society, library, William Troxell scrapbook, SCR 830.8, TROX.
19. See Bronner, *Following Tradition*; Bronner, "Shoemaker vs. Shoemaker."
20. Translation by author. See Preston Albert Barba's column, 'S Pennsylfawnisch Deitsch Eck, *Allentown Morning Call*, February 1, 1964.
21. Yoder, *Groundhog Day*, 43.
22. Patrick Donmoyer points out to me that *Dachs* is the Standard German word for "badger," which was watched in Germany for weather predictions; in America, Pennsylvania Germans turned to the groundhog.
23. Robert Kline tells me that the Deitsch term *dinda schlecker* describes a "brown noser" or "toady."
24. Fisher, "Solwell Files," 26–27.

25. Lehigh County Historical Society, library, Thomas Brendle scrapbook, SCR 830.8, BREN1.
26. This version is from the *Allentown Morning Call*, February 2, 1935, 5. Note alternative spelling here of "Pumpernickel" Bill.
27. *Allentown Morning Call*, editorial, February 3, 1941, 8.
28. *Allentown Morning Call*, February 2, 1971, 10.
29. I have never heard Deitsch spoken in the local Walmart, although I often hear Spanish. Sometimes I hear Deitsch at local farmers' markets.
30. A full version of this letter is found in Donner, "'Loss uns Deitscha wos m'r sin,'" 46–47.
31. I recently learned that there is an annual *Grundsau Lodsch fer Yunge* (groundhog lodge for the young) held at the Schwenkfelder Library and Heritage Center in Pennsburg (near the location of the Women's Lodge in East Greenville). This event appears to be for children to learn about heritage and groundhog lore, rather than a versammling. This region has many heritage activities, including the Women's Lodge, Groundhog Lodge #7, events sponsored by the Schwenkfelder Library and Heritage Center, and another very active heritage group, Goschenhoppen Historians Inc., which, among many other activities, sponsors an annual folklife festival.
32. When it was established, the Grossdaadi Lodge did not include the discontinued lodges in Philadelphia and Delaware. It also did not include the Women's Lodge in East Greenville, which was newly established and not widely known.
33. Schlegel, "Pennsylvania German Overhearers."
34. I am indebted to Paul Kunkel, who oversaw these programs for many years, for providing me with this information. There are other Deitsch-language classes sponsored by various other organizations, including historical societies, schools, and community organizations. Kutztown University sometimes offers Deitsch-language classes for college credit.
35. See *Allentown Morning Call*, October 5, 1989; October 7, 1989, B17.
36. Michael Werner of Germany and Patrick Donmoyer of the Pennsylvania Cultural Heritage Center at Kutztown University keep track of Pennsylvania German–language events in the newsletter *Hiwwe wie Driwwe*. This information about active versammlinge is found in an e-mail Werner sent, titled "Gehle Bledder 2010."
37. C. Stine, "Pennsylvania Germans and the School."
38. Kopp, *Phonology of Pennsylvania German English*. Kopp asserts that English was being used at the versammling in Lykens (ibid., 38), but a leading member of that lodge told me in 2013 that the meetings are almost entirely in Deitsch.
39. Donner, "Lingua Franca and Vernacular."
40. Peltz, *From Immigrant to Ethnic Culture*; Meek, "Respecting the Language of Elders"; see also Meek, *We Are Our*

Language; Grenoble and Whaley, *Saving Languages*.
41. Kopp, *Phonology of Pennsylvania German English*, 147.
42. For a discussion of Freemasonry in this region, see Donner, "Assimilation and Localism."
43. Clawson, *Constructing Brotherhood*, 14; Carnes, *Secret Ritual and Manhood*; Dumenil, *Freemasonry and American Culture*; Ferguson, *Fifty Million Brothers*.
44. For a discussion of these issues in Deitsch-language classes, see again Schlegel, "Pennsylvania German Overhearers."

Chapter 3

1. Troxell, "First Grundsow Lodge."
2. Snyder County Historical Society, library, Kerstetter Research and Work.
3. Kemp, *Pennsylvania German Versammlinge*, 191.
4. See, for example, Boyer, Buffington, and Yoder, *Songs Along the Mahantongo*; Brendle and Troxell, "Pennsylvania German Songs"; Buffington, *Pennsylvania German Secular Folk Songs*. For a discussion of the contemporary performance of Deitsch songs, see Yadush, "Current Trends of Dialect Preservation."
5. See Wikipedia entry, https://en.wikipedia.org/wiki/Schnitzelbank.
6. Keel, "A German-American Icon"; Keel, "Was ist eine Schnitzelbank?"
7. Fogel, *Beliefs and Superstitions*; Fogel, *Proverbs of the Pennsylvania Germans*.
8. Transcription and translation are from 2012 program of Lodge #1 and attributed to Will Warrkelholtz, "Will Rollingpin."
9. Again, although spelled *Leiver* and *Leiwer* in the programs, the word should be *Liever* or preferably *Liewer*. Such orthographic transpositions are common in writing Deitsch. My thanks to Robert Kline for pointing this out to me.

Chapter 4

1. I have seen this skit performed in other venues, notably by the Miller brothers at the Kutztown Folk Festival.
2. *Allentown Morning Call*, February 3, 1937, 6.
3. For a general discussion of Pennsylvania German plays, see Reichard, *Reichard Collection*; see also Fetterman, "Mosch Riehre." For discussions of *Asseba un Sabina*, see Yoder, *Discovering American Folklife*, 4; Fetterman, "*Asseba un Sabina*"; Langley, "*Asseba un Sabina*: The Culmination"; Langley, "*Asseba un Sabina*: Pennsylvania German Folk Identity"; Hanson, "*Nau sinn mer don redi*."
4. Fetterman, "Mosch Riehre," 54.
5. Buffington, introduction to Reichard, *Reichard Collection*, xxvii.
6. Ibid.
7. The original is in Deitsch; the translation was done by myself and Ron Treichler. The players are playing themselves; Julius Lentz, who wrote many of the future plays, has the role of the groundhog. A full version in Deitsch and English can be found in Donner and Treichler, "1934

Grundsow Skit." A copy of the original is in Thomas Brendle's scrapbook at the Lehigh County Historical Society, library, SCR 830.8, BREN 1.

8. *Allentown Morning Call*, February 3, 1972, 40.

9. *Allentown Morning Call*, February 3, 1936, 5. See also *New York Times*, March 27, 1904, SM8, for an early discussion of the goosebone method of predicting the weather in the Pennsylvania German region.

10. *Allentown Morning Call*, February 4, 1941, 21; see also *Allentown Morning Call*, February 3, 1939, 31.

11. Fetterman, "Die Grubbs Hiwwel Schul," 20.

12. Although originally written and performed thirty years earlier, the skit was performed again in 2013 when there was controversy concerning the Patient Protection and Affordable Care Act (Obamacare).

13. *Selinsgrove Times*, February 8, 1934, Snyder County Historical Society, library, Kerstetter Research and Work. The presentation seems to have been sarcastic and became widely popular (see *Selinsgrove Times*, January 28, 1937, Kerstetter Research and Work). The impersonation of Hitler was done by Fred Wentzel, director of education for the German Reformed Church, who was a popular speaker. The performance was done at the second annual meeting of the Selinsgrove Versammling. Hitler had been sworn in as chancellor of Germany only a year before the 1934 performance.

14. Lentz, "Schpiel."

15. *Allentown Morning Call*, February 3, 1973, 5.

16. *Allentown Morning Call*, February 4, 1975, 5, 7.

17. *Allentown Morning Call*, February 2, 1980, 11.

18. *Allentown Morning Call*, February 3, 1979 (Weekend).

19. *Allentown Morning Call*, February 3, 1949, 5.

20. *Allentown Morning Call*, February 3, 1966, 14; February 3, 1967, 7.

21. Recently, this versammling was discontinued because of dwindling numbers of Deitsch speakers.

22. See Haag, *Pennsylvania German Anthology*, 316–22.

23. Rourke, *American Humor*; Rourke, *Roots of American Culture*; Schleuter, "Theatrical Race"; Toll, "Folklore on the American Stage."

Chapter 5

1. See also Wieand, "Grundsau Lodge Meetings," 57.

2. Yoder, "Dialect Service," 11–12.

3. Gilbert, "Pennsylvania German Versammling Speeches," 6. This article is an excellent source for information about the versammlinge. See also Gilbert, "Religious Services," 279.

4. Gilbert, "Oratory of the Pennsylvania Germans," 191.

5. Ibid.

6. There is an excellent book about Rahn written by his daughter, Ruth C. (Rahn) Schaefer, *Rev. Clarence R. Rahn*.

7. Twain, *Mark Twain's Speeches*; Twain, *Mark Twain Speaking*; Will Rogers website, http://www.willrogers.com

/willrogers/radio/rp.html. Twain's later writings took a darker turn, and although they point to the general direction of American comedy in the twentieth century, they are quite distinct from the versammling humor, which is rooted in more optimistic traditions.

8. *Allentown Morning Call*, January 21, 1971, F1; Clarence Raymond Rahn Manuscript Collection (III), Evangelical and Reformed Historical Society.

9. Ron Treichler shared this passage with me; unfortunately, he passed away before this publication. I am grateful to Judy Miller for giving me permission to use this material. Ed Quinter proofread this passage, and I appreciate his suggestions for following the standardized conventions of the Buffington-Barba-Beam system.

10. *Allentown Morning Call*, February 3, 1956, 5; February 5, 1957, 15; February 3, 1960, 7; February 4, 1964, 5, 7; February 3, 1965, 5; February 3, 1966, 14; February 3, 1972, 5.

11. Rahn, "Rev. Clarence R. Rahn," 103, 104.

12. DeVoto, *Mark Twain's America*.

13. Twain, *How to Tell a Story*.

14. Wentz, "Parre Schtories."

15. Bronner, *Explaining Traditions*, especially chap. 8. For a view of this approach to German culture, see Dundes, *Life Is like a Chicken Coop*.

16. Blair and Hill, *America's Humor*, see especially 24, 66–73.

17. Ibid., 71–72.

18. Ibid., 158.

19. DeVoto, *Mark Twain's America*, 92–93.

20. Ibid., 93.

21. Discussions of these themes in Deitsch "dialect" literature can be found in Reichard, *Pennsylvania-German Dialect Writings*; Earl F. Robacker, *Pennsylvania German Literature*.

22. Bressler, "Pennsylvania German Wit," 19.

23. Ibid., 55.

24. Brodhead, *Cultures of Letters*; Jones, *Strange Talk*; Cmiel, *Democratic Eloquence*. Regional "local color" writers wrote about Pennsylvania Germans in English for a national audience, most notably Helen Martin, who used regional Pennsylvania German characters in a highly stereotyped and critical form, and Elsie Singmaster, who was far more complimentary of her Pennsylvania German characters. But neither of these authors wrote in the earthy, humorous tradition of Rauch and Harter that became important in versammling humor. Moreover, Martin and Singmaster, like all other regional writers, wrote exclusively in English; they were writing for a national audience and published in national books and magazines. See Martin, *Tillie, a Mennonite Maid*; Singmaster, *Heart Language*.

25. Blair and Hill, *America's Humor*, 363.

26. Fogel, *Beliefs and Superstitions*; Fogel, *Proverbs of the Pennsylvania Germans*.

27. 'S Pennsylfawnisch Deitsch Eck, *Allentown Morning Call*, February 5, 1938, translation by Ron Treichler; see Donner and Treichler, "Edwin Fogel's Grundsow."

28. Kloss, "German-American Language Maintenance," 221. For this reference I am indebted to Jennifer Schlegel; see Schlegel, "Pennsylvania German Overhearers," 145–46.

29. *Allentown Morning Call*, February 5, 1974, 7; February 1, 1975, 6.

Chapter 6

1. Wentz, "Henry Harbaugh, Quintessential 'Dutchman'"; Nolt, *Foreigners in Their Own Land*, 133–43.
2. Wentz, "Henry Harbaugh."
3. Harbaugh, *Harbaugh's Harfe*; Nolt, *Foreigners in Their Own Land*, 133–43; Reichard, *Pennsylvania-German Dialect Writing*, 54–73; Kieffer, *Henry Harbaugh*; Yoder, "Reformed Church."
4. Schaeffer, "Introduction," 5–6.
5. Simon Bronner describes the life of another Reformed pastor, Isaac Stiehly (1800–1869), who has many similarities to Harbaugh in his life and his support of heritage; see Bronner, "Elaborating Tradition."
6. See Reichard, *Pennsylvania-German Dialect Writing*.
7. Strasser, "1876 Centennial Monument"; C. Stine, "Pennsylvania Germans and the School."
8. Baer, "Berks County," 13; Horne, *Pennsylvania German Manual*; Donner, "'Neither Germans nor Englishmen'"; Donner, "First College Course in Pennsylvania German."
9. Croll, *Conrad Weiser and His Memorial Park*; Croll, *Annals of Womelsdorf*; Bradley, *Conrad Weiser Homestead*.
10. Swank, "From Dumb Dutch to Folk Heroes"; see especially 68–69.
11. Ibid.; Lord, "'Patriotism and Piety'"; Kammen, *Mystic Chords of Memory*, 218–19; Hellerich, "Founding of the Pennsylvania German Society"; Zimmerman, "Puritan and Cavalier."
12. Mercer, *Survival of the Mediaeval Art*; Mercer, *Bible in Iron*.
13. The museum at that time was called the Pennsylvania Museum and School of Industrial Art. It would soon become officially known as the Philadelphia Museum of Art.
14. Barber, *Tulip Ware*.
15. Rosenberger, *Pennsylvania Germans*, 147–51.
16. Downs, "House of the Miller"; Downs, "Pennsylvania German Galleries"; for a national perspective, see also Kammen, *Mystic Chords of Memory*, especially pt. 3, 299–527.
17. Nutting, *Pennsylvania Beautiful*; Weygandt, *Red Hills*; Yoder and Graves, *Hex Signs*; Donmoyer and Yoder, *Hex Signs*.
18. Robert Kline informs me that another reason behind the formation of the society was disagreements with the Pennsylvania German Society, which was still requiring members to prove they were descended from early German settlers. Eventually the two societies merged.
19. Yoder, "Pennsylvania Germans."
20. Rosenberger, *Pennsylvania Germans*, 181.
21. Iobst and Reichard, "*En Quart Millich*"; Fetterman, "Pennsylvania German Dialect Playwriting Contests."
22. Gilbert, "Religious Services in Pennsylvania German"; Yoder, "Dialect Service." It is possible that

some preachers gave sermons in Deitsch. Certainly, their Standard German sermons were influenced by their knowledge of Deitsch and English.
23. Blair and Hill, *America's Humor*; see especially 113–51. For an example of a recent liar's contest, see Breininger, "En Lieg beim Donnie Breininger."
24. Rosenberger, *Pennsylvania Germans*, 206–9.
25. See archives at Millersville University, McNairy Library, Special Collections, C. Richard Beam Collection, MS 145, file 43, box 3.
26. Hanson, "'*S Pennsylvaanisch Deitsch Eck.*"
27. Program, Pennsylvania German Folk Festival, June 26–27, 1936. For a discussion of folk festival events in Pennsylvania in the 1930s, see Gillespie, "Pennsylvania Folk Festivals."
28. See Lehigh County Historical Society, library, file PF 176 Trox 3.
29. For a discussion of these contests, see Fetterman, "Pennsylvania German Dialect Playwriting Contests."
30. See *Allentown Sunday Call–Chronicle*, September 3, 1944, 14. I am indebted to Don Breininger, who pointed out the importance of these events in the regional presentation of Pennsylvania German culture.
31. Yoder, "Twenty-Five Years of the Folk Festival."
32. Troxell, *Alta Neiyohrs-Winscha*; Troxell, *Aus Pennsylfawnia*; Brendle and Troxell, *Pennsylvania German Folk Tales*; Brendle and Troxell, "Pennsylvania Songs."
33. Most of the information in this paragraph comes from my interviews with Dr. Reverend Colonel Leonard Shupp and Brendle's daughter, Helen Milroy.
34. These books are kept at Historic Schaefferstown Inc., Schaefferstown, Pa. See Brendle and Beam, *Thomas R. Brendle Collection*, iv.
35. Ibid., ix (quotes in original).
36. Lick and Brendle, *Plant Names and Plant Lore*; Brendle and Unger, "Folk Medicine of the Pennsylvania Germans."
37. Reichard, *Reichard Collection*.
38. Brendle and Troxell, *Pennsylvania German Folk Tales*; Brendle, "Moses Dissinger."
39. The show did not come to an end because it was no longer popular. A person involved in its production had serious personal and legal problems that disturbed Rahn and led to the discontinuation of the show.
40. Again, for a general discussion of Pennsylvania German plays, see Reichard, *Reichard Collection*. For discussions of *Asseba un Sabina*, see Yoder, *Discovering American Folklife*, 4; Fetterman, "*Asseba un Sabina*"; Langley, "*Asseba un Sabina*: The Culmination"; Hanson, "*Nau sinn mer don redi*"; Langley, "*Asseba un Sabina*: Pennsylvania German Folk Identity."
41. Fetterman, "*Asseba un Sabina*," 57–58.
42. Langley, "*Asseba un Sabina*: Pennsylvania German Folk Identity."
43. *Lehighton Times News*, February 12, 1977, from Carl Snyder's scrapbook. Ruth Schaefer reports that the talk was at Lodge #6; Schaefer, *Rev. Clarence R. Rahn*, 18.

44. Yoder, "Reformed Church."
45. Rahn, "Pennsylvania German Humor."
46. Bronner, *Following Tradition*; Bronner, "Plain Folk and Folk Society."
47. Kammen, *Mystic Chords of Memory*, especially pt. 3, 299–527.
48. Rourke, *American Humor*.
49. DeVoto, *Mark Twain's America*.
50. *New York Times* (1851–2010), ProQuest Historical Newspapers. I admit that this is a rough measure. When I counted the numbers several years ago, the pattern was clearly similar, but the exact numbers were a little different.
51. Brendle and Troxell, "Pennsylvania German Songs," 63–64.

Chapter 7

1. See Bruner, *Cultures on Tour*; Kirshenblatt-Gimblett, *Destination Culture*; Smith, *Cultural Heritage*; Diamond, *American Aloha*; Handler and Gable, *New History in an Old Museum*; Bauman et al., *Reflections on the Folklife Festival*; Baron, "Sins of Objectification?" For a comprehensive review of Pennsylvania heritage sites, see Kitch, *Pennsylvania in Public Memory*.
2. Schmidt, *Consumer Rites*.
3. I recently heard that someone is trying to revive a Philadelphia lodge. The lodge in Delaware was also disbanded, but that lodge was different in organization and membership from the other lodges in its larger use of English and inclusion of women.
4. For recent discussions of language loss, see Fishman, *Handbook of Language*; Grenoble and Whaley, *Saving Languages*.
5. The concept of "ethnic identity" itself is time-bound. Social scientists did not start using the terms "ethnic identity" or "ethnic group" until well into the twentieth century. Gleason, "Identifying Identity"; Sollors, *Beyond Ethnicity*.
6. See Valuska and Donner, "Past and Future."

Glossary

Buffington-Barba-Beam standard spellings are followed by an asterisk.

Amtsleit*/Ombsleit	officers, of groundhog lodge board (*Raad*)
Brieder*	brothers, a common term used to describe the people at a groundhog lodge meeting
Deitsch*	Pennsylvania German / Dutch language
Deitsche (pl.), Deitscher (sing.)*	Pennsylvania Germans / Dutch
Ehrwatt	"word of honor," spoken toward the end of groundhog lodge meetings
Essa/Essta/Esse*	eat, food, dinner
Ferbinnerei/Verbinnerei*	binding, ceremonial oath or loyalty at groundhog lodge meetings
Fescht*	event, festival, special occasion
Fescht Rade	main speaker at versammlinge (*Feschtred**, banquet speech)
Fohrsinger/Vorsinger*	song leader
Formaischder/Formeschder/Vormeeschder*	leader, usually of general (non–groundhog lodge) versammlinge
Fraktur *	traditional Pennsylvania German calligraphy, usually on ceremonial certificates such as for baptism, marriage
Fuder Maischder/Meeschder*	food master, in charge of menu and food
Gabet/Gebet*	prayer
Gelthaver/Gelthewer	money holder, treasurer
Grossdaadi Lodsch*/Lodge	a group that oversees all the groundhog lodges (*Grossdaadi*, grandfather)
Grundsow/Grundsau*	groundhog
Haaptmann*/Habtmon	leader, the leader of a groundhog lodge
Lied* (sing.), Lieder (pl.)	song
Parre*	pastor, preacher

Raad*/Rawd	board of directors of a groundhog lodge; also a wheel
Rade	speaker; often refers to the main or *Fescht* speaker at meetings
Schnitzelbank	workbench; also the name of a popular song sung at Pennsylvania German gatherings
Schreiwer*/Schreiver	writer, secretary
Taufschein/Daafschein*	baptism certificate, often with calligraphy
Versammling*/Fersommling (sing.), Versammlinge*/Fersommlinge (plural)	gathering, meeting, a special event using the Deitsch language, including groundhog lodge meetings and non-groundhog general gatherings
Weibsleit*	women, women's group

Bibliography

Archival Sources

Evangelical and Reformed Historical Society, Lancaster Theological Seminary
Historic Schaefferstown, Inc.
Kutztown University, Rohrbach Library, archives
Lehigh County Historical Society, library
Millersville University, McNairy Library, Special Collections
Snyder County Historical Society, library
Ursinus College, Myrin Library

References

Baer, S. A. "Berks County." In *Report of the Superintendent of Public Instruction of the Commonwealth of Pennsylvania for the Year Ending June 1, 1876*, 13–18. Harrisburg: B. F. Meyers, 1876.

Barber, Edwin A. *Tulip Ware of the Pennsylvania-German Potters: An Historical Sketch of the Art of Slip-Decoration in the United States*. Philadelphia: Pennsylvania Museum and School of Industrial Art, 1903.

Baron, Robert. "Sins of Objectification? Agency, Mediation, and Community Self-Determination in Public Folklore and Cultural Tourism." *Journal of American Folklore* 123, no. 487 (2010): 63–91.

Bauman, Richard, Patricia Sawin, Inta G. Carpenter, Richard Anderson, Garry W. Barrow, William J. Wheeler, and Chong-sŭng Yang. *Reflections on the Folklife Festival: An Ethnography of Participant Experience*. Bloomington: Folklore Institute, Indiana University, 1992.

Beam, C. Richard, Joshua R. Brown, and Jennifer L. Trout. *The Comprehensive Pennsylvania German Dictionary*. Millersville: Center for Pennsylvania German Studies, Millersville University, 2004.

Blair, Walter, and Hamlin Lewis Hill. *America's Humor: From Poor Richard to Doonesbury*. New York: Oxford University Press, 1978.

Boyer, Walter E., Alfred Buffington, and Don Yoder, eds. *Songs Along the Mahantongo: Pennsylvania Dutch Folk-Songs*. Hatboro, Pa.: Folklore Associates, 1951.

Bradley, John. *Conrad Weiser Homestead*. Pennsylvania Trail of History Guides. Mechanicsburg, Pa.: Stackpole Books, 2001.

Breininger, Donald. "En Lieg beim Donnie Breininger." Transcribed and

translated by Ron Treichler. *Der Reggeboge* 39, nos. 1/2 (2005): 65–68.

Brendle, Thomas R. "Moses Dissinger, Evangelist and Patriot." In *William Rittenhouse and Moses Dissinger: Two Eminent Pennsylvania Germans*, by Milton Rubincam and Thomas R. Brendle, 91–192. Publications of the Pennsylvania German Society 58. [Scottdale, Pa.]: Pennsylvania German Society, 1959.

———. *The Thomas R. Brendle Collection of Pennsylvania German Folklore*. Edited by C. Richard Beam. Schaefferstown, Pa.: Historic Schaefferstown, 1995.

Brendle, Thomas R., and William S. Troxell. *Pennsylvania German Folk Tales, Legends, Once-Upon-a-Time Stories, Maxims, and Sayings Spoken in the Dialect Popularly Known as Pennsylvania Dutch*. Norristown, Pa.: Pennsylvania German Society, 1944.

———. "Pennsylvania German Songs." In *Pennsylvania Songs and Legends*, edited by George G. Korson, 62–128. Philadelphia: University of Pennsylvania Press, 1949.

Brendle, Thomas R., and Clyde Unger. "Folk Medicine of the Pennsylvania Germans: The Non-occult Cures." *Proceedings of the Pennsylvania German Society* 45 (1935): 1–303.

Bressler, Lee Albert. "Pennsylvania German Wit and Humor." M.A. thesis, Pennsylvania State University, 1943.

Brodhead, Richard H. *Cultures of Letters: Scenes of Reading and Writing in Nineteenth-Century America*. Chicago: University of Chicago Press, 1993.

Bronner, Simon J. "Elaborating Tradition: A Pennsylvania-German Folk Artist Ministers to His Community." In *Creativity and Tradition in Folklore: New Directions*, edited by Simon J. Bronner and W. F. H. Nicolaisen, 277–325. Logan: Utah State University Press, 1992.

———. *Explaining Traditions: Folk Behavior in Modern Culture*. Lexington: University Press of Kentucky, 2011.

———. *Following Tradition: Folklore in the Discourse of American Culture*. Logan: Utah State University Press, 1998.

———. "Plain Folk and Folk Society: John A. Hostetler's Legacy of the Little Community." In *Writing the Amish: The Worlds of John A. Hostetler*, edited by David L. Weaver-Zercher, 56–97. University Park: Pennsylvania State University Press, 2005.

———. "Shoemaker vs. Shoemaker: The Debate on Pennsylvania Germans in American Tradition." *Der Reggeboge* 30, nos. 1/2 (1996): 3–30.

Bruner, Edward M. *Cultures on Tour: Ethnographies of Travel*. Chicago: University of Chicago Press, 2005.

Buffington, Albert F. Introduction to Reichard, *Reichard Collection*, xix–xxviii.

———. "The Pennsylvania German Prose and Poetry of Thomas H. Harter and Harvey M. Miller." In

Something for Everyone—Something for You, 61–104.

———. *Pennsylvania German Secular Folksongs*. Breinigsville, Pa.: Pennsylvania German Society, 1974.

———. "Similarities and Dissimilarities Between Pennsylvania German and Rhenish Palatinate Dialects." Publications of the Pennsylvania German Society 3, 91–116. Breinigsville, Pa.: Pennsylvania German Society, 1970.

Buffington, Albert F., and Preston Albert Barba. *A Pennsylvania German Grammar*. Allentown, Pa.: Schlechter, 1954.

Carnes, Mark C. *Secret Ritual and Manhood in Victorian America*. New Haven: Yale University Press, 1989.

Clawson, Mary A. *Constructing Brotherhood: Class, Gender, and Fraternalism*. Princeton: Princeton University Press, 1989.

Cmiel, Kenneth. *Democratic Eloquence: The Fight over Popular Speech in Nineteenth-Century America*. New York: William Morrow, 1990.

Comaroff, John L., and Jean Comaroff. *Ethnicity, Inc.* Chicago: University of Chicago Press, 2009.

Croll, Philip C. *Annals of Womelsdorf, Pa. and Community, 1723–1923: History's Yard-stick for Two-hundred Years*. Reading, Pa., 1923.

———. *Conrad Weiser and His Memorial Park: A Little History in Three Parts*. Reading, Pa.: Reading Eagle Press, 1926.

DeVoto, Bernard. *Mark Twain's America*. Boston: Little, Brown, 1932.

Diamond, Heather A. *American Aloha: Cultural Tourism and the Negotiation of Tradition*. Honolulu: University of Hawai'i Press, 2008.

Donmoyer, Patrick J., and Don Yoder. *Hex Signs: Myth and Meaning in Pennsylvania Dutch Barn Stars*. Kutztown: Pennsylvania German Cultural Heritage Center, Kutztown University of Pennsylvania, 2013.

Donner, William W. "Assimilation and Localism: Some Very Small Towns in Mass Society." *Sociological Inquiry* 68, no. 1 (1998): 61–82.

———. "'Don't Shoot the Guitar Player': Tradition, Assimilation, and Change in Sikaiana Song Composition." *Journal of the Polynesian Society* 96 (1987): 201–21.

———. "The First College Course in Pennsylvania German." In *The Language and Culture of the Pennsylvania Germans: A Festschrift for Earl C. Haag*, edited by William D. Keel and C. Richard Beam, 15–26. Topeka, Kans.: Society for German-American Studies, 2010.

———. "'Loss uns Deitscha wos m'r sin': Leave Us Dutch the Way We Are; The Grundsow Lodges." *Pennsylvania German Review* (Spring 2002): 39–57.

———. "'Neither Germans nor Englishmen, but Americans': Education, Assimilation and Ethnicity Among Nineteenth-Century Pennsylvania Germans." *Pennsylvania History* 75, no. 2 (2008): 197–226.

———. "*Kastom* and Modernisation on Sikaiana." In "Custom Today," edited by Lamont Lindstrom and Geoffrey White, special issue, *Anthropological Forum* 6, no. 4 (1993): 541–56.

———. "Reply to Boyer, 'The Beautiful Truth'—Beauty Is in the Eye of the Beholder." *Pennsylvania German Review* (Spring 2003): 41–44.

———. "Research Note: Pennsylvania German Demographics." *Pennsylvania German Review* (Fall 2003): 41–51.

———. "'The Same Old Song but with a Different Meaning': Expressive Culture in Sikaiana Ethnic and Community Identity." In "The Arts and Politics of Oceania," edited by Karen Nero, special issue, *Pacific Studies* 15, no. 4 (1992): 67–82.

———. "'We Are What We Make of Ourselves': Abraham Reeser Horne and the Education of Pennsylvania Germans." *Pennsylvania Magazine of Biography and History* 124, no. 4 (2000): 521–46.

Donner, William W., and Ronald Treichler. "Edwin Fogel's Grundsow Speech of 1934." *Pennsylvania German Review* (Fall 2004): 18–20.

———. "1934 Grundsow Skit." *Pennsylvania German Review* (Spring 2004): 27–36.

Downs, Joseph. "The House of the Miller on the Millbach: The Architecture, Arts, and Crafts of the Pennsylvania Germans." 1929. Reprint, *Pennsylvania German Folklore Society* 1 (1936): 75–90.

———. "The Pennsylvania German Galleries in the Metropolitan Museum, New York." *Pennsylvania German Folklore Society* 1 (1936): 90–100.

Dumenil, Lynn. *Freemasonry and American Culture, 1880–1930*. Princeton: Princeton University Press, 1984.

Dundes, Alan. *Life Is like a Chicken Coop Ladder: A Portrait of German Culture Through Folklore*. New York: Columbia University Press, 1984.

Ferguson, Charles W. *Fifty Million Brothers: A Panorama of American Lodges and Clubs*. New York: Farrar and Rinehart, 1937.

Fetterman, William. "*Asseba un Sabina*: The Flower of Pennsylvania German Folk Theater." *Pennsylvania Folklife* 38, no. 2 (1988–89): 50–68.

———. "*Die Grubbs Hiwwel Schul im Lechaa Daal*: An Animal Play by Paul R. Wieand." *Historic Schaefferstown Record* 14, nos. 3/4 (1980): 19–39.

———. "*Mosch Riehre* (Stirring the Mush): The Influence of Playing Games in the Development of Pennsylvania German Folk Theatre." *Historic Schaefferstown Record* 22, no. 3 (1988): 35–56.

———. "The Pennsylvania German Dialect Playwriting Contests of 1941, 1942, 1983, and 1986." *Pennsylvania Folklife* 38, no. 2 (1989): 128–44.

Fisher, Ellwood. "Solwell Files: Dialect Selections and Translations by Melville J. Boyer." *Proceedings of the Lehigh County Historical Society* 28 (1970): 7–207.

Fishman, Joshua A., and Ofelia García. *Handbook of Language and Ethnic Identity*. Vol. 2, *The Success-Failure Continuum in Language and Ethnic Identity Efforts*. New York: Oxford University Press, 2011.

Fogel, Edwin M. *Beliefs and Superstitions of the Pennsylvania Germans*. Philadelphia: American Germanica Press, 1915.

———. *Proverbs of the Pennsylvania Germans*. Lancaster, Pa.: Pennsylvania-German Society, 1929.

Fogleman, Aaron Spencer. *Hopeful Journeys: German Immigration, Settlement, and Political Culture in Colonial America, 1717–1775*. Philadelphia: University of Pennsylvania Press, 1996.

Frantz, John B. "Franklin and the Pennsylvania Germans." *Pennsylvania History* 65, no. 1 (1988): 21–34.

Giddens, Anthony. *The Consequences of Modernity*. Stanford: Stanford University Press, 1990.

Gilbert, Russell Wieder. "The Oratory of the Pennsylvania Germans at the Versammlinge." *Susquehanna University Studies* 4, no. 3 (1951): 187–213.

———. "Pennsylvania German Versammling Speeches." *Pennsylvania Speech Annual* 13 (1956): 3–20.

———. "Religious Services in Pennsylvania German." *Susquehanna University Studies* 5 no. 4 (1956): 277–89.

Gillespie, Angus K. "Pennsylvania Folk Festivals in the 1930s." *Pennsylvania Folklife* 26, no. 1 (1976): 2–11.

Gleason, Philip. "Identifying Identity: A Semantic History." *Journal of American History* 69, no. 4 (1983): 910–31.

Grenoble, Lenore A., and Lindsay J. Whaley. *Saving Languages: An Introduction to Language Revitalization*. Cambridge: Cambridge University Press, 2006.

Haag, Earl C., ed. *A Pennsylvania German Anthology*. Selinsgrove: Susquehanna University Press, 1988.

Handler, Richard, and Eric Gable. *The New History in an Old Museum: Creating the Past at Colonial Williamsburg*. Durham: Duke University Press, 1997.

Hanson, Gregory J. "*Nau sinn mer don redi fer die Wascht tzu schtuppe*—Making Sausage with Asseba and Sabina: A Reflection of Pennsylvania German Folk Life." *Der Reggeboge* 43, no. 2 (2009): 13–26.

———. "'*S Pennsylvaanisch Deitsch Eck*: A Journalistic Success Story." *Der Reggeboge* 43, no. 1 (2009): 21–32.

Harbaugh, Henry. *Harbaugh's Harfe: Gedichte in Pennsylvanisch-Deutscher Mundart*. Edited by Benjamin Bausman. Philadelphia: Reformed Church Publication Board, 1870.

Harter, Thomas H. *Boonastiel: A Volume of Legend, Story, and Song in

"Pennsylvania Dutch." Bellefonte, Pa.: Keystone Gazette, 1904.

Hellerich, Mahlon. "The Founding of the Pennsylvania German Society." *Der Reggeboge* 25, no. 2 (1991): 33–41.

Hohman, Johann G., and Patrick J. Donmoyer. *Der Freund in der Noth, Or, the Friend in Need: An Annotated Translation of an Early Pennsylvania Folk-Healing Manual*. Kutztown: Pennsylvania German Cultural Heritage Center, Kutztown University of Pennsylvania, 2012.

Horne, Abraham R. *Pennsylvania German Manual, for Pronouncing, Speaking, and Writing English: A Guide Book for Schools and Families*. Kutztown, Pa.: Urick and Gehring, 1875.

Iobst, Clarence F., and Harry H. Reichard. "*En Quart Millich un en Halb Beint Raahm*": A Pennsylvania German Comedy. Allentown, Pa.: Pennsylvania German Folklore Society, 1939.

Jones, Gavin. *Strange Talk: The Politics of Dialect Literature in Gilded Age America*. Berkeley: University of California Press, 1999.

Kammen, Michael G. *Mystic Chords of Memory: The Transformation of Tradition in American Culture*. New York: Knopf, 1991.

Kazal, Russell A. *Becoming Old Stock: The Paradox of German-American Identity*. Princeton: Princeton University Press, 2004.

Keel, William D. "A German-American Icon: *O, du schöne Schnitzelbank!*" *Yearbook of German-American Studies* 38 (2003): 221–53.

———. "Was ist eine Schnitzelbank? The Tradition Behind the Popular German-American Sing-Along." *Missouri Folklore Society Journal* 24 (2002): 21–35.

Kemp, Alvin F. *The Pennsylvania German Versammlinge*. Allentown, Pa.: Pennsylvania German Folklore Society, 1944.

Kieffer, Elizabeth C. *Henry Harbaugh, Pennsylvania Dutchman, 1817–1867*. Norristown, Pa.: Norristown Herald, 1945.

Kirshenblatt-Gimblett, Barbara. *Destination Culture: Tourism, Museums, and Heritage*. Berkeley: University of California, 1998.

Kitch, Carolyn. *Pennsylvania in Public Memory: Reclaiming the Industrial Past*. University Park: Pennsylvania State University Press, 2012.

Kloss, Heinz. *The American Bilingual Tradition*. Rowley, Mass.: Newbury House, 1977.

———. "German-American Language Maintenance Efforts." In *Language Loyalty in the United States: The Maintenance and Perpetuation of Non-English Mother Tongues by American Ethnic and Religious Groups*, edited by Joshua Fishman, 206–52. The Hague: Mouton, 1966.

Kopp, Achim. *The Phonology of Pennsylvania German English as Evidence of Language Maintenance and Shift*. Selinsgrove: Susquehanna University Press, 1999.

Kraybill, Donald B. *The Riddle of Amish Culture*. Baltimore: Johns Hopkins University Press, 2001.

Kraybill, Donald B., and Carl Bowman. *On the Backroad to Heaven: Old Order Hutterites, Mennonites, Amish, and Brethren*. Baltimore: Johns Hopkins University Press, 2002.

Kraybill, Donald B., and James P. Hurd. *Horse-and-Buggy Mennonites: Hoofbeats of Humility in a Postmodern World*. University Park: Pennsylvania State University Press, 2006.

Kraybill, Donald B., and Steven M. Nolt. *Amish Enterprise: From Plows to Profits*. Baltimore: Johns Hopkins University Press, 1995.

Lambert, Marcus Bachman. *A Dictionary of the Non-English Words of the Pennsylvania-German Dialect*. Allentown, Pa.: Pennsylvania German Society, 1924.

Langley, Zachary. "*Asseba un Sabina*: Pennsylvania German Folk Identity in an American World." M.A. thesis, Pennsylvania State University, 2010.

———. "*Asseba un Sabina*: The Culmination of a Folk Culture Movement." *Der Reggeboge* 43, no. 2 (2009): 3–12.

Lentz, Julius E. "Schpiel: Sie Fange Der Hitler." Edited by C. Richard Beam. *Historic Schaefferstown Record* 19, no. 3 (1985): 39–51.

Lick, David E., and Thomas R. Brendle. *Plant Names and Plant Lore Among the Pennsylvania Germans*. Lancaster, Pa.: The Society, 1923.

Lord, Mary. "'The Patriotism and Piety of Our Fathers': The Origins of the Pennsylvania German Society as a Nineteenth Century Hereditary Organization." *Der Reggeboge* 42, no. 2 (2008): 29–40.

Louden, Mark L. "The Development of Pennsylvania German Linguistics Within the Context of General Dialectology and Linguistic Theory." In *A Word Atlas of Pennsylvania German*, by Lester W. J. Seifert, 7–52. Madison, Wis.: Max Kade Institute for German-American Studies, 2001.

———. *Pennsylvania Dutch: The Story of an American Language*. Baltimore: Johns Hopkins University Press, forthcoming.

Lynd, Robert S., and Helen M. Lynd. *Middletown: A Study in Contemporary American Culture*. New York: Harcourt, Brace, 1929.

Martin, Helen R. *Tillie, a Mennonite Maid: A Story of the Pennsylvania Dutch*. New York: Century, 1904.

Meek, Barbra A. "Respecting the Language of Elders: Ideological Shift and Linguistic Discontinuity in a Northern Athapascan Community." *Journal of Linguistic Anthropology* 17, no. 1 (2007): 23–43.

———. *We Are Our Language: An Ethnography of Language Revitalization in a Northern Athabascan Community*. Tucson: University of Arizona Press, 2010.

Mercer, Henry C. *The Bible in Iron: Or, the Pictured Stoves and Stove Plates of the Pennsylvania Germans; with Notes on Colonial Fire-Backs in the United States, the Ten-Plate Stove, Franklin's Fireplace and the Tile Stoves of the Moravians in*

Pennsylvania and North Carolina, Together with a List of Colonial Furnaces in the United States and Canada. Doylestown, Pa.: Bucks County Historical Society, 1914.

———. *The Survival of the Mediaeval Art of Illuminative Writing Among Pennsylvania Germans.* Doylestown, Pa.: Bucks County Historical Society, 1897.

Miller, Richard. *Pennsylvania German Groundhog Lodges.* Pamphlet. N.d.

Musser, Dorothy. "The Life and Work of Thomas H. Harter." M.A. thesis, Pennsylvania State University, 1932.

Nolt, Steven M. *Foreigners in Their Own Land: Pennsylvania Germans in the Early Republic.* University Park: Pennsylvania State University Press, 2002.

Nutting, Wallace. *Pennsylvania Beautiful (Eastern).* Framingham, Mass.: Old America, 1924.

Parsons, William. *The Pennsylvania Dutch: A Persistent Minority.* Boston: Twayne, 1976.

Rahn, Clarence R. "Pennsylvania German Humor." In *Intimate Glimpses of the Pennsylvania Germans: Proceedings*, edited by Homer T. Rosenberger, 43–54. Waynesboro, Pa., 1966.

———. "Rev. Clarence R. Rahn." In *A Pennsylvania-Dutch Dictionary*, 101–4. Quakertown, Pa.: Meredith, n.d.

Reichard, Harry H. *Pennsylvania-German Dialect Writings and Their Writers: A Paper Prepared at the Request of the Pennsylvania-German Society.* Lancaster, Pa.: Press of the New Era Print. Co., 1918.

———. *The Reichard Collection of Early Pennsylvania German Dialogues and Plays.* Edited by Albert F. Buffington. Lancaster: Fackenthal Library, Franklin and Marshall College, 1962.

Robacker, Earl F. *Pennsylvania German Literature: Changing Trends from 1683 to 1942.* Philadelphia: University of Pennsylvania Press, 1943.

Rosenberger, Homer T. *The Pennsylvania Germans, 1891–1965, Frequently Known as the "Pennsylvania Dutch"; Seventy-Fifth Anniversary Volume of the Pennsylvania German Society.* Lancaster: Pennsylvania German Society, 1966.

Rourke, Constance. *American Humor: A Study of the National Character.* New York: Harcourt, Brace, 1931.

———. *The Roots of American Culture and Other Essays.* Edited by Van Wyck Brooks. New York: Harcourt, Brace, 1942.

Schaefer, Ruth C. *Rev. Clarence R. Rahn: Country Preacher, Humorist, and Philosopher.* Pennsylvania German Society, Legacy Series, no. 4. Ephrata: Pennsylvania German Society, 2014.

Schaeffer, Nathan C. "Introductory." In *The Life of the Rev. Henry Harbaugh, D.D.*, by Linn Harbaugh, 5–19. Philadelphia: Reformed Church Publication Board, 1900.

Schlegel, Jennifer R. "Pennsylvania German Overhearers: Living with Language Maintenance and Language

Loss." Ph.D. diss., University of California, Los Angeles, 2004.

Schleuter, Jennifer. "'A Theatrical Race': American Identity and Theatrical Performance in the Writings of Constance M. Rourke." *Theatre* 60 (2008): 529–54.

Schmidt, Leigh E. *Consumer Rites: The Buying and Selling of American Holidays*. Princeton: Princeton University Press, 1995.

Shoemaker, Alfred Lewis, Don Yoder, and William Woys Weaver. *Christmas in Pennsylvania: A Folk-Cultural Study*. Mechanicsburg, Pa.: Stackpole Books, 2009.

Singmaster, Elsie. *Heart Language: Elsie Singmaster and Her Pennsylvania German Writings*. Edited by Susan Colestock Hill. University Park: Pennsylvania State University Press, 2009.

Smith, Laurajane. *Cultural Heritage: Critical Concepts in Media and Cultural Studies*. 4 vols. London: Routledge, 2007.

Sollors, Werner. *Beyond Ethnicity: Consent and Descent in American Culture*. New York: Oxford University Press, 1986.

Something for Everyone—Something for You = Ebbes fer Alle—Ebber Ebbes fer Dich: Essays in Memoriam Albert Franklin Buffington. Publications of the Pennsylvania German Society 14. Breinigsville, Pa.: Pennsylvania German Society, 1980.

Stine, Clyde S. "The Pennsylvania Germans and the School." In *The Pennsylvania Germans*, edited by Ralph Wood, 105–27. Princeton: Princeton University Press, 1942.

Stine, Eugene S. *Pennsylvania German Dictionary: Pennsylvania German–English, English–Pennsylvania German*. Birdsboro, Pa.: Pennsylvania German Society, 1996.

Strasser, Brendon D. "The 1876 Centennial Monument at Kutztown: An Enduring Symbol of Pennsylvania German Ethnic Pride." *Pennsylvania German Review* (Spring 2002): 25–38.

Swank, Scott T., ed. *Arts of the Pennsylvania Germans*. New York: Published for the Henry Francis du Pont Winterthur Museum by W. W. Norton, 1983.

———. "From Dumb Dutch to Folk Heroes." In Swank, *Arts of the Pennsylvania Germans*, 61–76.

———. "Henry Francis du Pont and Pennsylvania German Folk Art." In Swank, *Arts of the Pennsylvania Germans*, 77–101.

Toll, Robert C. "Folklore on the American Stage." In *Handbook of American Folklore*, edited by Richard M. Dorson, 247–56. Bloomington: Indiana University Press, 1983.

Troxell, William S. *Alta Neiyohrs-Winscha: Nei Ousgewa fom Pumpernickle Bill*. Allentown, Pa.: The author, 1933.

———, ed. *Aus Pennsylfawnia: An Anthology of Translations into the Pennsylvania German Dialect*. Philadelphia: University of Pennsylvania Press, 1938.

———. "The First Grundsow Lodge." Reprinted from the *Allentown*

Morning Call in *Pennsylvania Dutchman* 4, no. 12 (1953): 4.

Twain, Mark. *How to Tell a Story, and Other Essays*. New York: Harper and Brothers, 1897.

———. *Mark Twain Speaking*. Edited by Paul Fatout. Iowa City: University of Iowa Press, 1978.

———. *Mark Twain's Speeches*. New York: Harper and Brothers, 1910.

Valuska, David L., and William W. Donner. "The Past and Future of the Pennsylvania German Language: Many Ways of Speaking German; Many Ways of Being American." In *Globalization and the Future of German*, edited by Andreas Gardt and Bernd Huppauf, 229–42. Berlin: Mouton de Gruyter, 2004.

Waldenrath, Alexander. "The German Language Newspress During World War I." *Pennsylvania History* 42, no. 1 (1975): 25–41.

Weaver, William W. *As American as Shoofly Pie: The Foodlore and Fakelore of Pennsylvania Dutch Cuisine*. Philadelphia: University of Pennsylvania Press, 2013.

Weber, Samuel E. *The Charity School Movement in Colonial Pennsylvania*. 1905. Reprint, New York: Arno Press, 1969.

Wentz, Richard E. "Harbaugh: Heemweh un' Himmel." *Der Reggeboge* 41, no. 2 (2007): 33–42.

———. "Henry Harbaugh, Quintessential 'Dutchman.'" *Pennsylvania Folklife* 41, no.1 (1991): 36–47.

———. "Parre Schtories." *Pennsylvania Folklife* 40, no. 1 (1990): 24–35.

Werner, William. "The Revival of Interest in Pennsylvania German, 1927–1937." 'S Pennsylfawnisch Deitsch Eck, *Allentown Morning Call*, December 11 and 18, 1937.

Weygandt, Cornelius. *The Red Hills: A Record of Good Days Outdoors and In, with Things Pennsylvania Dutch*. Philadelphia: University of Pennsylvania Press, 1929.

Wieand, Paul R. "Grundsau Lodge Meetings." *Historic Schaefferstown Record* 16, no. 4 (1982): 51–60.

Wood, Ralph Charles, ed. *The Pennsylvania Germans*. Princeton: Princeton University Press, 1943.

Yadush, Chantel Lynn. "Current Trends of Dialect Preservation Through Musical Performance in the Pennsylvania German Community of Southeastern Pennsylvania." M.A. thesis, University of Maryland, 2008.

Yoder, Don. "The Dialect Service in the Pennsylvania German Culture." *Pennsylvania Folklife* 27, no. 4 (1978): 2–13.

———. *Discovering American Folklife: Studies in Ethnic, Religious, and Regional Culture*. Ann Arbor, Mich.: UMI Research Press, 1990.

———. *Groundhog Day*. Mechanicsburg, Pa.: Stackpole Books, 2003.

———. "Palatine, Hessian, Dutchman: Three Images of the German in America." In *Something for Everyone—Something for You*, 107–29.

———. *The Pennsylvania German Broadside: A History and Guide*. University Park: Pennsylvania

State University Press for the Library Co. of Philadelphia and the Pennsylvania German Society, 2005.

———. "The Pennsylvania Germans: Three Centuries of Identity Crisis." In *America and the Germans: An Assessment of a Three-Hundred-Year History*, vol. 1, *The Relationship in the Twentieth Century*, edited by Frank Trommler and Joseph McVeigh, 42–65. Philadelphia: University of Pennsylvania Press, 1985.

———. "The Reformed Church and Pennsylvania German Identity." *Der Reggeboge* 26, no. 2 (1992): 1–16.

———. "Twenty-Five Years of the Folk Festival." *Pennsylvania Folklife* 23, Folk Festival Supplement (1974): 2–7.

Yoder, Don, and Thomas E. Graves. *Hex Signs: Pennsylvania Dutch Barn Symbols and Their Meaning*. Mechanicsburg, Pa.: Stackpole Books, 2000.

Zimmerman, Thomas C. "Puritan and Cavalier? Why Not the Pennsylvania-German?" *Proceedings of the Pennsylvania German Society* 1 (1891): 36–47.

Index

Der Airscht Pennsylfawnish Deitscher Picknick (the First Pennsylvania German Picnic), 29
alcohol, 59
Allentown folk festival, 110
Allentown Morning Call, 32–33, 35–37, 87–88, 109–10, 119
"America," 49
Americanization, 22, 107–8
American popular culture, 99–100, 120–22
American society, Pennsylvania German interactions with, 107–8
Anabaptists, 13–15, 40, 118, 134 n. 4
apple butter, 87
"Apple Butter Days," 110
Asseba un Sabina, 66, 115

Baer, Samuel, 103
baptism certificate, 28, fig. 12
Barba, Preston, 18, 29, 42, 95, 109, 119
Barber, Edwin Atlee, 105
Beam, C. Richard, 18, 112
Benton, Thomas Hart, 120–21
Berks County Fersommling, 30
Binding as oath of membership, 53, figs. 3, 4, 23
Blair, William, 91–92, 93–94
Breininger, Don, 73, 84, 88, 89–90
Brendle, Thomas, 55, 58, 67–69, 111–13, 117, 121
Bressler, Lee, 93
Bronner, Simon, 91, 119–20
Buffington, Albert, 18, 66–67, 76, 119

Buffington-Barba-Beam system, 17–18
burglaries, 86–87

Candlemas, 32–33
Church people, 13, 40, 133 n. 4
church services, 108
Clawson, Mary Ann, 44
Clinton, Bill, 75, fig. 29
common people
    emphasized in Rahn's speeches, 81
    public and intellectual fascination with, 120–21
Croll, Philip C., 103
current events, 9, 70–71, 74

Deitsch, 15–18
    classes on, 38, 129, 138 n. 34
    development of, as literary language, 100–102
    egalitarianism created through, 44
    enjoyment of, 45
    expressiveness of, 88–90
    importance of, in versammlinge, 48, 129
    loss of, 19–20, 26, 39–41, 127
    origins of, humor, 90–94
    plays in, 65–66
    referred to as dialect, 135 n. 8
    spelling in, 17–18, 135 n. 12, 139 n. 9
Deitsch-language events, 27, 29, 30, 108–9, 129
Deitsch literature, 16–17, 93, 102
Delaware lodge, 37

DeVoto, Bernard, 89, 92–93, 120
dialectizers, 107–8
dialect(s)
    Deitsch as, 17, 135 n. 8
    regional, 93, 137 n. 8
dinner, 53–54
Dissinger, Moses, 113
Donmoyer, Patrick, 134 n. 4
Downs, Joseph, 106
du Pont, Henry Francis, 106

East Greenville lodge, 37–38
education, Deitsch in, 103
eiron, 91–92, 102
energy crisis, 71
English, 48, 129
En Quart Millich un en Halb Beint Raahm (Iobst), 66, 108
ethnic identity
    defined, 6
    of German Americans, 22–23
    of Pennsylvania Germans, 25–26, 100–104, 130–31
    use of term, 144 n. 5
ethnicity, 6

Fetterman, William, 65, 66, 69, 115
fines, for using English, 48
Fisher, Ellwood D., 33–34
flag, Pennsylvania German, 38–39, fig. 13
Fogel, Edwin, 58, 94–95
folk culture, public and intellectual fascination with, 106, 120–21
folk festivals, 110–11, 121
    Allentown folk festival, 110
    Kutztown Pennsylvania Dutch Folk Festival (*also* Kutztown Folk Festival), 111, 119, 133 n. 4
Folk Medicine of the Pennsylvania Germans: The Non-occult Cures (Brendle and Unger), 112–13

food, 53–54
"Die Ford Maschien," 55
Fords, 55
Franklin, Ben, 22, 136 n. 17
fraternal organizations, 43–44, 137 n. 17
Freemasons, 43, 44, 137 n. 17

Geissinger, David, 37
German immigrants, versus Pennsylvania Germans, 12
Germanizers, 107–8
German Reformed Church, 101–2, 114, 117, 134 n. 3
Gershwin, George, 120
Giddens, Andrew, 20
Gilbert, Russell, 29, 42, 80
Gladfelter, Millard, 37
"goosebone man," 69
Grossdaadi Lodge (Grandfather Lodge), 38, 138 n. 32
Groundhog Day, 31–33, 36–37
Groundhog Lodge #1
    activities of, 35–36, 37, 125–26
    admission ticket for, fig. 11
    band at, fig. 20
    baptism certificate of, fig. 12
    board members wheel, fig. 17
    board of, 31, fig. 22
    broadside of, 74, fig. 9
    conclusions and last words, 59
    decor of, 64, figs. 14–16
    first meeting of, 53, fig. 1
    formation and influence of, 4
    main speeches given at, 87–88
    meeting announcement and invitation of, fig. 10
    meeting of, fig. 18
    oath of membership at, 53, figs. 3, 23
    performances at meetings of, 57
    preparations for meeting of, 48
    procession at, 49, fig. 21

programs for meetings of, 49–60, figs.
 6, 8, 24–29
purpose of, 34
solemn minute at, 52
theatricality at, 64–65, figs. 33, 34
women protest for entry into, 71, fig. 31
Groundhog Lodge #2
 board of, fig. 2
 oath of membership at, fig. 4
 performers at, fig. 32
Groundhog Lodge #3, 37
Groundhog Lodge #16, 65, fig. 35
groundhog lodges
 critics of, 94–96
 defined, 2
 first meeting, 28
 future of, 39
 history and activities of, 30–39
 officers of, 31
 origins of, 26
 for young, 138 n. 31
groundhog(s)
 brought across Jordan Creek, fig. 35
 ceremony for bringing in, 49, fig. 21
 crowning, fig. 5
 as food, 34, 53
 as icon of Pennsylvania German identity, 94
 legend regarding, 31–34
 in lodge decor, figs. 14–16
 in past and present, 34
 procession for, 49 fig. 21
 in skits, 67–69
 weather prediction of, 57
Guardian, 100, 102

Harbaugh, Henry, 100–102
Harter, Thomas H., 28, 102
Heffendrager, Clarence, 86–87, 89
Heffentrager, Leroy, 54
Heintzelman, Russell, 116

heritage
 academic views on, 20–22
 defined, 6
 evolution of, 125
heritage events, 20–22, 125, 127–28
High German, 15–16
Hill, Hamlin Lewis, 91–92, 93–94
Hitler, Adolf, 70–71, 140 n. 13, fig. 8
Die Hoffning (Brendle), 113
Horne, Abraham Reeser, 103
humor
 critics of, 94–96
 ethnic, 44–45
 in main speech, 79, 80, 86
 origins of Deitsch, 90–94
 in program covers, 74–75
 reflects themes in Pennsylvania German and American writing, 5, 90–94
 and theatricality, 63–64, 66–67, 68, 69–70, 73–74
 of versammlinge, 127

Iobst, Clarence, 66, 108

Kammen, Michael, 120
Kaska, 41
Kazal, Russell, 22–23
Keel, William, 56
Kemp, Alvin, 30, 42, 52
Kern, Lucy, 38
Kline, Robert, 84–85, 115
Klinger, Irwin, 73–74
Kloss, Heinz, 95
Kopp, Achim, 40
Kunkel, Paul, 85
Kutztown monument, 103
Kutztown Pennsylvania Dutch Folk Festival
 (*also known as* Kutztown Folk Festival), 111, 119, 133 n. 4

Landis, George, 105–6
Landis, Henry Kinzer, 105–6
Langley, Zach, 115
language. *See also* Deitsch; English
    loss of, 41
    revival of, 129
Leisy, Elmer L., 87
Lewinsky, Monica, 75, fig. 29
"liar's contests," 108–9
lodge business, 56–57
Louden, Mark, 134 n. 1
Lutheran Church, 114, 117

main speech
    Clarence Rahn and, 81–88
    and expressiveness of Deitsch, 88–90
    at lodge meetings, 58
    and origins of Deitsch humor, 90–94
    requirements for, 79–80
Marcellus shale deposits, 72
Martin, Helen, 141 n. 24
Masons, 43, 44, 137 n. 17
Meck, Bill, 65, 69–70, 72–73, fig. 33
membership oath. *See* Binding
men, as versammlinge organizers, 42–43
Mercer, Henry, 105
Miller, Richard, 26, 85
Milroy, Helen, 111
Moravians, 134 n. 3
"Mule Ears," 81–83
music, 54–56
Die Mutter (Brendle), 113

"New Year's Wish," 74, fig. 9
Nolt, Steven, 22, 100
Nutting, Wallace, 107

oath of membership. *See* Binding
Obama, Barack, 71, 137 n. 9
Old Order Amish, 13–15, 40

past, in skits, 67, 69–70, 71–72, 76
pastors, jokes about, 91
patriotism, 49–52, 100
Pennsylvania Dutch, 10–12. *See also*
    Pennsylvania Germans
Pennsylvania-German, 103
Pennsylvania German flag, 38–39, fig. 13
Pennsylvania German Folklore Society, 104,
    107. *See also* Pennsylvania German
    Society
Pennsylvania Germans, 10–15, 20
    changes experienced by, 18–20
    changing lives of, 126–27
    culture of, 22–23, 25–26, 99–100
    distorted perception regarding, 3–4
    ethnic identity of, 25–26, 100–104,
        130–31
    future of, 128–31
    groundhog as icon of, 94
    heritage events of, 21
    interest in material culture of, 104–8
    language and culture of, 12–13, 15–18
    leaders in expression of heritage of,
        109–18
    "local color" writings on, 141 n. 24
    origins of humor of, 90–94
    revival of interest in, 2, 26–27, 99–100
    scholarship regarding, 118–20
    settlements of, 14
    traditions of, 10
    traits of, 87
    versammlinge as expression of
        identity of, 2–3
Pennsylvania German Society, 11, 12, 104,
    106
*Plant Names and Plant Lore Among the
    Pennsylvania Germans* (Brendle
    and Lick), 112–13
Pledge of Allegiance, 49–52
powwowing, 71
prayer(s)

of Clarence Rahn, 85
   at lodge meetings, 52–53
presidential elections, 71
program covers, 74–75, figs. 6, 8, 24–29
public education, Deitsch in, 103
Pumpernickle Bill. *See* Troxell, William
Punxsutawney Phil, 69, 72, 88

Rahn, Clarence
   background of, 90
   crowning groundhog, fig. 5
   on Deitsch, 88
   on importance of versammlinge, 3
   influence of, on future main speakers, 5, 84, 87
   as leader in expressing Pennsylvania German heritage, 113–18
   as main speaker, 79–80, 81–88
   on sensible nonsense of lodge activities, 3, 95
   speaking at Groundhog Lodge #1, fig. 30
   speaking at Groundhog Lodge #2, fig. 7
redware pottery, 105
Reformed Church. *See* German Reformed Church
regional writing and dialects, 93, 137 n. 8
Reichard, Harry Hess, 29, 65, 119
Rogers, Will, 81, 120
Roosevelt, Franklin, 28
Rosenberger, Homer, 108
Rourke, Constance, 75–76, 120

Schaefer, Richard, 117
Schaefer, Ruth, 84, 90
Schaeffer, Nathan, 101
Schlegel, Jennifer, 38, 135 n. 8
"Schnitzelbank," 55–56, fig. 19
Schwenkfelders, 134 n. 3
"Sect" people, 13, 134 n. 3. *See also* Anabaptists
sexual innuendo, 43, 80

Shoemaker, Alfred, 32, 119
Silfer, Franklin, 87
singing, 54–56. *See also* "Schnitzelbank"
Singmaster, Elsie, 141 n. 24
skits, 63–65
   audiences of, 70
   current events in, 70–71
   at Groundhog Lodge #1, fig. 34
   at Groundhog Lodge #2, fig. 32
   at lodge meetings, 57
   origins of, 65–66, 75–77
   patterns in, 66–67
   production of, 73–74
   themes in, 67–69, 71–73
Snyder, Carl, 26, 38, 45, 63, 89
Snyder, Gilbert, 109
solemn minute, 52
songs, 54–56. *See also* "Schnitzelbank"
speeches. *See* main speech
spontaneity, in skits, 64, 65
Standard German. *See* High German
Stine, Clyde, 39

tall tales, 108–9
theatricality. *See* skits
thirteen, significance of, 137 n. 17
Toll, Robert, 76
traditional songs, 54–56. *See also* "Schnitzelbank"
travel books, 107
Troxell, William
   on admission to groundhog lodge, 48
   compiles Deitsch folk songs, 55
   as humorous Deitsch writer, 102
   inspired by interest in regional folklore, 121
   as key versammlinge organizer, 28–29, 30–31
   as leader in expressing Pennsylvania German heritage, 109–11, 117
   as main speaker, 58

Troxell, Willoughby, 69
Twain, Mark, 81, 89, 90, 92–94, 120, 140–41 n. 7

union churches, 114
University of Delaware, 37

versammling(e)
    awareness of, 2
    beginnings of, 27–30
    and changing lives of Pennsylvania Germans, 126–27
    critics of, 94–96
    defined, 9
    Deitsch in, 20, 48
    development of, 122
    and events in American history, 125–26
    as example of American cultural development, 13
    as expression of ethnic identity, 2–3
    first, attended by author, 1–2
    first recorded, 14
    format and structure of, 47, 49–60, 125
    future of, 39, 128–31
    officers of, 31
    participation in, 41–45
    preparation for, 47–48
    significance of, 9–10
    unique aspects of, 127–28
    variations of, 2
    and view about present-day life, 127

Walking Purchase, 71
weather prediction
    at lodge meetings, 57
    in skits, 68–69, 71–72
Weaver, William Woys, 134 n. 1
Weiser, Conrad, 103
Wentz, Richard, 91, 100
Weygandt, Cornelius, 107

Wolf, Richard, 85
women
    admittance of, to lodges, 129, fig. 31
    in skits, 66, 71
women's lodge, 37–38
Wood, Grant, 120–21
Woodruff, John, 27–28, 29, 42
"Word of Honor," 58–59

Yiddish, 41
Yoder, Don, 29, 33, 80, 107, 117, 119

Zimmerman, Sterling, 87–88

Serious Nonsense